D1478902

SCATTER MY DARKNESS

SCATTER MY DARKNESS

Turning Night to Day with the Gospel

Fr. John Henry Hanson, O. Praem.

Published by Scepter Publishers, Inc.
info@scepterpublishers.org
www.scepterpublishers.org
800-322-8773
New York

Cover art: Magdalene with the Smoking Flame by Georges de La Tour (1593-1652) / Alamy.com

Cover design: Studio Red Design

Text design and pagination: Studio Red Design

Library of Congress Control Number: 2021937655

ISBN

Paperback: 978-1-59417-424-7

eBook: 978-1-59417-425-4

Printed in the United States of America

TABLE OF CONTENTS

Lord, kindle a light for my guidance and scatter my darkness.

—LITURGY OF THE HOURS, ANTIPHON FOR PSALM 18

PREFACE

Lord, now lettest thou thy servant depart in peace, according to thy word; for mine eyes have seen thy salvation which thou hast prepared in the presence of all peoples, a light for revelation to the Gentiles, and for glory to thy people Israel.

—LUKE 2:29-32

Simeon's words—the *Nunc Dimittis*—reveal the grace that flooded his soul when he held the Christ Child, the Light and Savior of the world, in his arms (see Jn 8:12). A faithful and prayerful man, Simeon persevered in blessed hope that before his death, he would see the "consolation of Israel… the Lord's Christ," and he did (Lk 2:25,26).

Simeon's praise and thanksgiving to God is rich in references to the Old Testament. "[All] the ends of the earth shall see the salvation of our God," the prophet Isaiah foretells (Is 52:10), and he describes the Savior as "a light to the nations, to open the eyes that are blind, to bring out the prisoners from the dungeon, and from the prison those who sit in darkness" (Is 42:6,7). The psalmist prays, "There are many who say, 'O that we might see some good. Lift up the light of thy countenance upon us, O Lord!'" (Ps 4:6). The prophecies and the desires of the human heart have been fulfilled in Jesus Christ. God has kept his promise.

In the natural order, we need light to live and to flourish. We depend on the sun, over which we exercise no control. Our dependence on light for existence points to the sun as a sign or symbol of the divine. Pope Benedict wrote, "Earthly light is the most direct reflection of God's reality and gives us our best glimpse of him who dwells in unapproachable light."[1]

Grace elevates or perfects nature, as St. Thomas Aquinas teaches. The Catholic liturgy makes use of light to lift our minds and hearts to Heaven. During Advent, we refer to the coming Savior as the "Daystar" or the "Oriens" or the "Radiant Dawn," all signifying that light that comes into the world from the East, first in nature and then in grace. We can think of Candlemas, for instance, which commemorates the Presentation of the Child Jesus in the Temple, where Simeon encountered him. The Gospel for that Mass includes the text we have been considering from Luke 2. For Compline, or Night Prayer, the Church has adopted the *Nunc Dimittis* as the final Gospel canticle in the daily Divine Office. Finally,

1 Joseph Ratzinger (Pope Benedict XVI), *Dogma and Preaching: Applying Christian Doctrine to Daily Life* (San Francisco: Ignatius Press, 2011), p. 295.

we recall the *Exultet sung by the deacon to the Paschal Candle at the Easter Vigil: "This is the night that with a pillar of fire banished the darkness of sin."*

The drama of salvation history recounts the contest between light and darkness. St. John tells us, "God is light and in him is no darkness at all" (1 Jn 1:5). In God was life, "and the life was the light of men" (Jn 1:4). Sin, however, entered the world through the disobedience of Adam and Eve, and so did men love "darkness rather than light, because their deeds were evil" (Jn 3:19).

Fr. John Henry Hanson, O. Praem. understands well this drama, both as a spiritual writer and a priest with a fine pastoral sense. While he knows that light and darkness contend with each other in the world and even in the Church, he also knows that this contest first takes place in the souls of believers who wish to be "children of the light" (Eph 5:7). In *Scatter My Darkness,* Fr. John Henry offers practical counsel and encouragement for those who seek the *Lumen Gentium,* "the Christ, the Son of God, he who is coming into the world" (Jn 11:27), and who desire above all the grace that Simeon received: the peace of soul that only Jesus Christ can give (see Jn 14:27).

Fr. John Henry marks this path to the light who is Christ because he has followed it himself and continues to be faithful to its challenges and to be the grateful beneficiary—not unlike Simeon—of its marvelous rewards. In his abundant priestly charity, he reminds us of the great things to which the Good God has called us, but he remains keenly aware of the tangle of the human heart (see Jer 17:9) and how we can frustrate our own longing for salvation and eternal life. He urges us not to let our human weakness be an obstacle to grace, but rather the condition through which God works to make us pleasing to Him, to make us holy. The more we depend on grace and the more we cooperate with it, the more the mind and heart will be enlightened and strengthened by Christ. "He who does what is true comes to the light that it may be clearly seen that his deeds have been wrought in God" (Jn 3:21).

Fr. John Henry confirms, as the light of the Gospel itself directs, that what we have received as a gift, we are to share as a gift, in turn, with others (see Mt 10:8). Let's return one more time to the liturgy of the Great Vigil of Easter. We receive a small flame—which brings to mind the light we first received at Baptism—and then we pass it along to those near us, a small but strong symbol of God's wise plan for how the light of grace spreads in a world made dark and dangerous by sin. "The light shines in the darkness, and the darkness has not overcome it" (Jn 1:5). Through light—once again, in nature and in grace—we come to see and to know ourselves and others, and we see that Christ continues to keep His promises: that He is present among His children, that we might "give glory to [our] Father who is in Heaven" (Mt 5:16).

As in all things, we look to Our Lady, "Star of the New Evangelization," as St. John Paul II described her, to bring us to her Son in this world and to the light of glory for eternity. Fr. John Henry points us to Our Lady, who "looks forth like the dawn, fair as the moon, bright as the sun, terrible as an army with banners" (Song 6:10). Mary, Mother of God and our Blessed Mother, embodies our hope, stills our fears, and makes our prayers to Jesus perfect and complete, so that His light may shine in our hearts.

Raymond Leo Cardinal Burke
Shrine of Our Lady of Guadalupe
La Crosse, WI
August 15, 2021
Solemnity of the Assumption of the Blessed Virgin Mary

INTRODUCTION
Setting the Stage

In the liturgical experience, Christ the Lord is the light which illumines the way and reveals the transparency of the cosmos.

—ST. JOHN PAUL II[1]

othing says drama like a stage and curtains, just as nothing says liturgy like an altar, candles, and incense. The connection between drama and liturgy is not as random as might first appear and is certainly germane to the subject of this book. The following pages will explore the many ways in which Christ gives us light to scatter the darkness in our lives, but before peering into both the light and the darkness, we need to know why we need light in the first place. Why are dark places in my life at all, and how do Christ's love and grace dissipate them?

---

1   John Paul II, Apostolic Letter to the Bishops, Clergy, and Faithful to Mark the Centenary of Orientalium Dignitas of Pope Leo XIII Orientale Lumen (May 2, 1995), 11. Vatican website: http://www.vatican.va.

Here is where the stage and the curtain and the altar interface.

The Divine Liturgy of the Armenian Catholic Church, an Eastern Rite I am privileged to celebrate regularly, features an *ad orientem* (east-facing) altar noticeably elevated by several rows of platforms and steps, surrounded by ornamental processional torches, with metal liturgical fans encircled by bells. As the celebrant faces the altar, behind him hangs a large red velvet curtain, roughly twenty feet in length, which closes during certain points of the liturgy. It is particularly what that curtain does during Lent, what it conceals and reveals, that inserts us into the spirit of the following reflections.

During "Great Lent" Armenian Catholics enact a highly symbolic gesture in drawing that massive, rich curtain across the sanctuary for most of the sacred liturgy. The congregation can hear the prayers and chants, but can see none of the ritual movements and gestures. That you can't see the familiar unfolding of the rites is naturally disconcerting—not to mention frustrating.

But the point of this "dramatic" sign is precisely to underscore the disconcerted and frustrated state we are in after original sin. With an angel stationed at Eden's entrance to guard the garden with flaming sword, we have no direct access to God after the Fall. This state is forcefully conveyed by the thematic title of the Second Sunday of Great Lent in the Armenian Church: "Sunday of the Expulsion." The tragedy of our first parents' expulsion from Paradise is commemorated, providing a liturgical bookend for the coming redemption celebrated at Easter.

The state of affairs after original sin is one of hard labor, weakness, ignorance, frustration, fear, and especially alienation from God and neighbor. That is, until Christ comes.

If St. Paul reminds us of this state of separation, of being "separated from Christ, alienated from the commonwealth of Israel, and strangers to the covenants of promise, having no hope and without God in the world" (Eph 2:12), it is to relieve us (like a dramatic catharsis) by announcing the gospel reversal:

> But now in Christ Jesus you who once were far off have been brought near in the blood of Christ. For he is our peace, who has made us both one, and has broken down the dividing wall of hostility, by abolishing in his flesh the law of commandments and ordinances, that he might create in himself one new man in place of the two, so making peace, and might reconcile us both to God in one body through the cross, thereby bringing the hostility to an end. And he came and preached peace to you who were far off and peace to those who were near; for through him we both have access in one Spirit to the Father. (Eph 2:14–18)

The tension of our fallen state finds resolution in Christ, just as when the curtains part and reveal the sanctuary alive with ritual gesture, noble vestments, and God's presence among us in the Bread of Life. What has happened is the unveiling of what had always been there, but that we were prevented from seeing until Christ comes to break through the barrier.

With this book, I hope to part the curtains on our lives to reveal the presence of God in ways and places that we had never seen him before. The Lord is never absent, but his presence demands eyes that want to see, want to discern his unique action in a still-fallen—but redeemed—world. This demands a retraining of the inner eye to perceive the world as God wants us to see it.

> The eye is the lamp of the body. So, if your eye is sound, your whole body will be full of light; but if your eye is not sound, your whole body will be full of darkness. If then the light in you is darkness, how great is the darkness! (Mt 6:22–23)

Since, as Jesus says, either light or darkness can envelope the whole person, it is crucial that we let in the holy light and use it as our lamp to see by. Following St. John Paul II, I am going to propose the liturgy as the lens that trains us to see the divine richness of life in this world. Christ, the Light of the World, truly makes the created order (the cosmos) transparent in the Divine Liturgy, a perspective we are meant to take with us into the workaday world, finding God in our lives and in our environment.

And although the liturgy of the Latin Church meets the senses with its own variety of sounds and scents, it is more characteristic of the Eastern liturgies to employ symbols, melodies, and visuals to more dramatic effect. "This sense of the inexpressible divine reality," writes St. John Paul II, "is reflected in liturgical celebration, where the sense of mystery is so strongly felt by all the faithful of the Christian East."[2] As the holy Pontiff goes on to say so beautifully:

> ...liturgical prayer in the East shows a great aptitude for involving the human person in his or her totality: the mystery is sung in the loftiness of its content, but also in the warmth of the sentiments it awakens in the heart of redeemed humanity. In the sacred act, even bodiliness is summoned to praise, and beauty, which in the East is one of the best loved names expressing the divine harmony and the model of humanity transfigured, appears everywhere: in the shape of the church, in the sounds, in the colors, in the lights, in the scents. The lengthy duration of the celebrations, the repeated invocations, everything expresses gradual identification with the mystery celebrated with one's whole person. Thus the prayer of the Church already becomes participation in the heavenly liturgy, an anticipation of the final beatitude.[3]

Our whole self becomes bathed in the light of Christ, with no part of our sense-life left untouched, unmoved by the divine. And it is precisely the misuse of our senses that

2 John Paul II, Orientale Lumen, 6.
3 John Paul II, Orientale Lumen, 11.

often darkens our minds and clouds our vision.

The sacred liturgy, informed as it is by Sacred Scripture and the ancient prayers of the Church, is a place of concentrated light. Thus, in these pages, the Bible, liturgical prayer, and the saints will guide us to see both where we are in the dark, as well as the unique light with which Christ scatters that darkness. For it is Christ who becomes the very curtain of the sanctuary by opening his flesh for us in sacrifice, the one and only sacrifice for which the liturgy exists at all:

> Therefore, brethren, since we have confidence to enter the sanctuary by the blood of Jesus, by the new and living way which he opened for us through the curtain, that is, through his flesh, and since we have a great priest over the house of God, let us draw near with a true heart in full assurance of faith, with our hearts sprinkled clean from an evil conscience and our bodies washed with pure water. (Heb 10:19–22)

And how fitting it is that baptism has from biblical times been called "illumination" or "enlightenment." Many Armenian churches, in fact, including the cathedral where I serve, are named after St. Gregory "the Illuminator," the saintly bishop who baptized the pagan king of Armenia in AD 301, making Armenia the first officially Christian nation in the world.

Water and light both cleanse: one outwardly, the other inwardly. The light of Christ is cleansing grace for the soul.

"Having the eyes of [our] hearts enlightened" (Eph 1:18), we are enabled to see the hope to which we have been called, and that hope is the light that will guide our walk from darkness to light, from this side of the veil to the place where Christ dwells in glory.

CHAPTER ONE
Called Out:
Why Budge from the Shadows?

But you are a chosen race, a royal priesthood, a holy nation, God's own people, that you may declare the wonderful deeds of him who called you out of darkness into his marvelous light.

—1 PETER 2:9

Futuristic, dystopian novels such as Huxley's *Brave New World* and Bradbury's *Fahrenheit 451* often feature dehumanized people living in a mechanized, utilitarian, results-oriented world. The beauty of nature or of art are no longer objects of interest because beauty is not considered functional or useful. It is all about efficient production; the *how* of things, not the *why* of things. A teenage girl in Ray Bradbury's novel is disparaged by the story's antagonist on this very point: she thwarts her high school education, he complains, by being more interested in knowing *why* something is done than *how*.

The *how* is all about the steps, the process that leads to the product. The *why* unearths the motive behind the steps. Even if our own culture exhibits many of the dysfunctional signs of futuristic tales, we should be wary of letting the *how* mentality infiltrate our spiritual life. To approach the life of the spirit with a results-oriented mindset is to upset the order of things: the spiritual life is first and last a relationship God initiates with me and the life he makes grow within me.

Results, or fruits, are by no means negligible, but they don't augment the spiritual life in the same way that practicing music scales or building muscle produces musical virtuosity and strength over time. No one has a personal relationship with a musical instrument or with any other activity. With the Lord, relational give-and-take displaces the practice-makes-perfect approach better suited to hobbies. The spiritual life is no more a hobby than is married life.

The *how* and the *why* genres of spiritual books are both necessary. We all have to begin somewhere, and might as well begin with a first step that leads to another. Order is vital in the spiritual life, and for those beginning to pray or struggling to overcome some fault, knowing what to do here and now is crucial. And yet, it is misleading to view the spiritual life merely as a series of steps terminating in holiness. Following steps is not the same as following the Lord, as the apostles found out time and again. Remember how Jesus answered one of the ultimate *how* questions ever uttered in Scripture:

> Thomas said to him, "Lord, we do not know where you are going; how can we know the way?" Jesus said to him, "I am the way, and the truth, and the life; no one comes to the Father, but by me." (Jn 14:5–6)

St. Thomas gets no to-do list, but something infinitely better: a reintroduction to his Savior, seated not more than a couple of feet from him. In a sense, it is a *why* answer to a *how* question. St. Thomas wants something practical to do, some directions to follow, but Jesus reminds him why he is following at all: St. Thomas has already found the way because Jesus has drawn him to himself. So what is St. Thomas doing wrong? Is his question so out of line?

It's not out of line; neither is it difficult to relate to his insistence on touching the wounds of Jesus post-resurrection. But St. Thomas is in a hurry to know and see things, and the Lord wants him to slow down and contemplate, to see the Father speaking and acting through the Son. The way and the Lord are inseparable: you will know the way to go the more deeply you know the Lord. "If you had known me, you would have known my Father also" (Jn 14:7). Jesus will not excuse his disciples from contemplation. His parables and many of his other teachings will find no home in us without our willingness to sit with them in prayer. Only then are they fully plumbed and owned. We cannot scroll through the Scriptures and get anything like good fruit unless we let the seed of the Word of God enter and germinate in the soil of our hearts.

We've gone from futuristic novels to gospel dialogues to spiritual seeds simply to stress the essential priority of grace in the spiritual life, a needed reminder in a point-and-click, do-it-yourself culture. Progress and growth must be present, and steps must be covered, yet it is God who begets in us any desire to do good in his name (see Phil 2:13). He calls first, and grace always accompanies the call, raising us powerfully from complacency, fear, or doubt to follow the way to new life.

Now God has called each one of us out of darkness. For the moment, we will set aside the specific nature of that darkness, whether it takes a moral, psychological, or spiritual form. In the end, the call is fundamentally the same: to live in the freedom of the children of God, unhindered by sin, uncompromised by the very trials our lives impose on us. That is, no matter what the darkness is, we shouldn't regard it as a permanent obstacle to our happiness, to our ability to follow Christ wholeheartedly. But to get to that point where we can even acknowledge the possibility of rising from darkness is the work of hope, a grace God never fails to offer and which the devil always seeks to extinguish.

Does the Book of Job fairly describe your state of soul?

Therefore snares are round about you,
and sudden terror overwhelms you;

your light is darkened, so that you cannot see,
and a flood of water covers you. (Jb 22:10–11)

This sounds like an ambush. And until someone clears away these snares, parts the clouds, and makes the waters recede, forward progress comes to a halt. Like the feeling of being surrounded or of drowning, darkness oppresses and terrifies.

Yet there is one about whom Scripture testifies, he "delivered me from all my fears" and "even the darkness is not dark to thee, the night is bright as the day; for darkness is as light with thee" (Ps 34:4; 139:12). This is the One who frees from the snare, rides on the clouds, and walks upon the waters. And he, not darkness, is ultimately the subject of this book, for he is the Light of the World.

[T]he words of Jesus explaining his identity and his mission are so important: "I am the light of the world; whoever follows me will not walk in darkness, but will have the light of life" (Jn 8:12).

Our personal encounter with Christ bathes life in new light, sets us on the right path, and sends us out to be his witnesses. This new way of looking at the world and at people, which comes to us from him, leads us more deeply into the mystery of faith, which is not just a collection of theoretical assertions to be accepted and approved by the mind, but an experience to be had, a truth to be lived, the salt and light of all reality[1]

Resources abound that offer guidance for people who feel lost or in darkness—whether that means depression, addiction, or general anxiety about the meaning of life. However helpful they may be for those seeking light, if they fail to identify Christ as the true Light that enlightens everyone, they fail on the most important point. Because in the end, a search for light is not like browsing through any other section in a bookstore: self-help, gardening, games, or fiction. Each have their own audience, but the "audience" for light is not a particular readership. It is fallen humanity. It is all of us. And the fact that so many people are searching for light in our time may strike at least one positive note: getting fed up with worldly solutions to problems of the soul shows openness to something better and greater than this world can offer.

When all your paths have run into dead ends, the unexplored suddenly seems more promising. You are open to light, coming not from the tried and familiar places, but from somewhere formerly unsearched: "For it is the God who said, 'Let light shine out of darkness,' who has shone in our hearts to give the light of the knowledge of the glory of God in the face of Christ" (2 Cor 4:6).

St. Paul relates the creation of light with knowing Christ

1 John Paul II, Message of the Holy Father to the Youth of the World on the Occasion of the XVII World Youth Day (Toronto, July 25, 2002), 3. Vatican website: www.vatican.va.

Jesus intimately in our hearts, and that is enormous for those in darkness. To see the glory of God shining in the face of Christ is to see hope in human form! Precisely because God has taken a glorious and human face that yet endures fist blows, lacerations, and spitting, an astonishing truth dawns upon on us: he feels what we feel and knows our experience from the inside.

> For by his incarnation the Son of God has united Himself in some fashion with every man. He worked with human hands, He thought with a human mind, acted by human choice and loved with a human heart. Born of the Virgin Mary, He has truly been made one of us, like us in all things except sin.[2]

Nothing so encourages us in trouble as the face of a beloved person who knows our struggle, sympathizes, and whose support lifts us out of our rut. The beautiful dynamic of mother and son as it transpires at the fourth Station of the Cross could not be more apposite or poignant: a look, maybe not even a caress, but a look of intense love is all we need to redouble our courage and carry on to the end.

Our culture has turned its face away from Christ. He will always be, as Isaiah prophesies, "one from whom men hide their faces," despised and disrespected (Is 53:3). This is because the look on that sacred face convicts, even as it

2   Second Vatican Council, Pastoral Constitution on the Church in the Modern World *Gaudium et Spes* (December 7, 1965), 22. Vatican website: www.vatican.va.

consoles. St. Peter went out and wept bitterly over his betrayal of the Lord after a brief eye contact with him: "And the Lord turned and looked at Peter. [...] And he went out and wept bitterly" (Lk 22:61–62). Christ's look is as simple and penetrating as that. Not everyone wants to engage it. Those who turn away will never find true light.

Light, like truth, is confrontational by nature. It exposes reality as it is. And reality can be ugly and shocking, demanding difficult choices of us. Not everyone wants that. People might seek a vague, inner enlightenment in the hopes of reaching equilibrium and calm, connectedness to nature, and so on. That is all fine, as far as it goes. But it is not the light that Christ gives. St. Paul identifies his goal in preaching the gospel as producing a very specific fruit: "love that issues from a pure heart and a good conscience and sincere faith" (1 Tim 1:5). It is *Christ the light* that purifies heart and conscience; it is faith that trusts in the power of God—and not our own insight—to do that otherwise impossible inner cleansing.

Our cultural turning away from Christ is reflected in the dire moniker given by St. John Paul II to the modern milieu: *culture of death*. It is one that kills its own. Instead of fostering human life, it runs people ragged until they are no longer useful, no longer profitable. If culture consists of a particular view of the human person and his or her purpose, the right ordering of society, moral and aesthetic values, and unspoken assumptions about how things ought to go, then a deathly culture is one with both homicidal and suicidal tendencies. It is all pointless tunneling to no goal, with no light to look forward to on the other side.

When people start to feel useless, worthless, and hopeless, they have taken up residence in a place Scripture calls "a land of deep darkness" (Is 9:2). Get enough people together without purpose, bereft of gospel morality and of hope, and suddenly you have a culture sitting "in darkness and in the shadow of death" (Lk 1:79), with no way out.

A Personal Problem

Darkness might take different sociological forms, but in the end, it is a universal personal problem. Everyone must traverse a land of shadows before reaching the marvelous light of Christ. "For once you were darkness," runs St. Paul's categorical judgment, "but now you are light in the Lord" (Eph 5:8). "Having no hope and without God in the world" is also how St. Paul categorizes people before coming to know Christ, further referring to them as "alienated" and "strangers" (See Eph 2:12).

The before-and-after contrast between life without Christ and life in him justifies these stark judgments. If "Christ is life" (Col 3:4), then the absence of Christ, or the rejection of him, must mean death. Our contention in these pages is that Christ, the Light of the World, will never dim, never be anything other than the One whose "face was like the sun shining in full strength" when St. John saw him in heaven (Rev 1:16). He will always be the true Light that enlightens each of us in the most important ways.

It is far too easy to get dazzled and distracted by all the other lights in the world. Whether it is a fascinating network of city lights, the dim lighting of a nightclub, or even the celebrities whom we call "stars," our fascination with all that glitters knows no satiety. Our minds are like crows, Thomas Merton once observed, picking up "everything that glitters, no matter how uncomfortable our nests get with all that metal in them."[3] It's an image of people weighed down and uncomfortable, but lacking a brighter light to go by, wanting a word that mysteriously doubles as a lamp for our steps.

The Christian soul, indeed every human soul, is made for more than an eye-catching shimmer. The light that Christ gives is a divine fire—a fire cast upon the earth, never burning out, but consuming us in love as it inevitably sends us on mission.

St. Josemaría Escrivá sees our status as children of God as synonymous with this mission, the Lord's own command to let our light "shine before men" (Mt 5:16).

We are children of God. —Bearers of the only flame that can light up the paths of the earth for souls, of the

---

3   Thomas Merton, *New Seeds of Contemplation* (New York: New Directions, 1961), 104.

only brightness which can never be darkened, dimmed or overshadowed.

—The Lord uses us as torches, to make that light shine out... It depends on us that many should not remain in darkness, but walk instead along paths that lead to eternal life.[4]

We have to learn how to give ourselves, to burn before God like the lamp placed on a lampstand to give light to those who walk in darkness; like the sanctuary lamps that burn by the altar, giving off light till they are consumed.[5]

Torch bearers, burning lamps—that is what we become once we let the Lord rescue us from the power of darkness and give us his light.

Giving thanks to the Father, who has qualified us to share in the inheritance of the saints in light. He has delivered us from the dominion of darkness and transferred us into the kingdom of his beloved Son. (Col 1:12–13)

Although this book is not a study of literary motifs, of the biblical use of light and darkness from Genesis to Revelation, the fact that they often intermingle in the major events of our redemption gives us more than a little to think about. The interface is unmistakable at the most significant moments of

---

4   Josemaría Escrivá, *The Forge* (New York: Scepter, 2002), 1.

5   Escrivá, *The Forge*, 44.

the Lord's earthly life—from his birth by night in Bethlehem to Judas' nighttime betrayal to the darkness that covered the land upon Jesus' death on the cross.

Yet the night sky of the Lord's birth was infiltrated and overrun by the luminous apparition of choral angels, and the shadows of Good Friday were soon evaporated by the dawn of Easter Sunday. All of which is another way of saying that although Jesus was not received by his own, yet the Light of the World shone in the darkness and the darkness could not overcome it, although it furiously tried to suppress the Light, run interference against his teaching, even snuff him out in death. Yet the flame reignites. The sun rises again. The phoenix of ancient myth shakes off the dead ashes and spreads its wings anew.

God is calling us out of darkness and into his marvelous light. And why? We've got a story to tell of what he has done for us, a mission to *declare the wonderful deeds of him who called us.* That declaration is every Christian's mission, as we seek to be lights shining in a dark world, like the first streaks of dawn signaling the sun that never sets (see 2 Pt 1:19).

CHAPTER TWO
First Steps into the Light

Whoever is in darkness which is not thick, goes forward, especially when he
hopes to find light. But anyone bewildered by thick darkness stands still.

—ST. THOMAS AQUINAS[1]

If something is broken, but still usable, after a while you might stop noticing the defect. Like a key that fits into a lock, though you have to jiggle it to make it turn, you adjust yourself to the broken thing and treat it as practically normal. Or some household appliance that only works if you tilt it in this or that direction: you just do what's necessary, virtually forgetting its flaw. During my years of

---

1   Thomas Aquinas, *Latin-English Edition of the Works of St. Thomas Aquinas,* Vol. 33, *Commentary on the Gospel of Matthew: Chapters 1-12,* trans. Jeremy Holmes and Beth Mortensen, ed. The Aquinas Institute (Lander, Wyoming: The Aquinas Institute for the Study of Sacred Doctrine, 2013), no. 357, p. 115. Paraphrased for clarity. "For he who from the beginning is in a darkness which is not thick, and so he is not stupefied by it, goes forward, and most of all when he hopes to find light; and when he is stupefied by the darkness, he stands still."

theology studies in Rome, I memorized which cobblestones on the street wobbled and which trapped rain water, stepping on or around them as though playing hopscotch; the rhythm of my gait accommodated itself to the unevenness of the path.

People who have walked, dwelt, and sat in a place of shadows and gloom begin to take the darkness for granted. Hopelessness is a given. Broken is their normal. The contrast between night and day is no longer perceived or perhaps even perceptible to them. Rendering St. Thomas Aquinas differently: *Darkness immobilizes a person who has no hope of finding light.*

But imagine yourself in a crowd of beaten-down, discouraged people living under foreign occupation, paying taxes to an emperor you've never seen. You've grown used to being oppressed, used to having no voice, resigned to a life that will never be free—functional, yes, but never life at its fullest. As you stand in that crowd, imagine a noble-looking man in your midst solemnly comissioning you:

> You are the light of the world. A city set on a hill cannot be hid. Nor do men light a lamp and put it under a bushel, but on a stand, and it gives light to all in the house. Let your light so shine before men, that they may see your good works and give glory to your Father who is in heaven. (Mt 5:14–16)

Something about his voice authorizes him to speak so confidently, and you to take it all seriously. The One who speaks sees light in you, as though he himself put it there to shine out, to attract, to glorify. And so it is.

As you take your first steps in this newfound confidence, you find the light bathing you an unfamiliar, yet welcome, pool. Yet you might wonder how to move about without too much awkwardness. Racking your brain, you try to remember how to celebrate the springtime or how to sing harvest songs. Or, since you have come out on the losing end so many times, you puzzle over how to declare victory and share the spoils. And what about peace? So long you've been feeding on wartime rations, so geared for conflict that you must relearn how to breathe freely and feast at a banquet prepared in the sight of your foes.

The prophet Isaiah foretells a time when all these possibilities will be realities:

> The people who walked in darkness
>> have seen a great light;
> those who dwelt in a land of deep darkness,
>> on them has light shined.
> Thou hast multiplied the nation,
>> thou hast increased its joy;
> they rejoice before thee
>> as with joy at the harvest,
>> as men rejoice when they divide the spoil.
> For the yoke of his burden,
>> and the staff for his shoulder,

the rod of his oppressor,

thou hast broken as on the day of Midian.

For every boot of the tramping warrior in battle tumult

and every garment rolled in blood

will be burned as fuel for the fire.

For to us a child is born,

to us a son is given;

and the government will be upon his shoulder. (Is 9:2–6)

If the mere thought of rejoicing—of even knowing what to rejoice over—has given way to simply coping, Isaiah envisions a time when all that makes us feel trapped and weighed down like a beast of burden will be lifted and dissolved. And because the birth of this "child" heralds that prophesied time, should it surprise us to discover that the time for rejoicing and liberation has already come and will never again pass away?

Isaiah records as an accomplished fact what had seemed to be wishful thinking in his day. At a remove of two thousand years, then, does it feel like we've missed something essential about Christ's mission and our own? Does it even put us in the position of the prodigal son's elder brother, needing to be reminded of the unique riches we already possess?

Like many things in Scripture, we don't really *hear* something unless we're particularly open to it. Our Lord compares us to people who drink either old or new wine, cautioning those prejudiced against the new precisely because it *is* new: "No one after drinking old wine desires new; for he says, 'The old is good'" (Lk 5:39). Yes, good enough. But how strangely resistant we can be when the better comes along. If we can't discern the better from the good, or if we fear the better simply because it's novel, we need to recall what we were born for.

In a previous book, I quoted one of the favorites sayings of the Venerable Mother Luisita of the Most Blessed Sacrament, O.C.D.: "For greater things you were born." Well, greater than what? Greater than what we can imagine, greater than what we think is great. We were born for what no eye has seen, nor ear heard, nor heart conceived. People are often willing to settle for far less and call it a day. The old and worn is better.

Greater means something that goes beyond our ability to understand, to see, to appreciate. How can we see and appreciate the end of the road while we are still traveling on it? Often when we enjoy the good things of this life, we think, *this must be it*. To be valued by those around us, to accomplish things that make us stand out and to be applauded for them, this must be it. Or to indulge in something pleasurable, repeatedly, this must be our destination.

We were born not for vainglory, nor to see our name in lights, nor to have our ego or flesh gratified—but for greater things. If we are born for greater things, can we possibly expect to see that, much less hold it in the palm of our hands?

"Now hope that is seen is not hope. For who hopes for what he sees? But if we hope for what we do not see, we wait for it with patience" (Rom 8:24–25).

The possibility that something fresh and unknown could be better than the familiar good is scarcely entertained, even if it is the new and eternal testament, even if it is living the new life in Christ.

Putting on the new nature (see Eph 4:24), clothing ourselves with Christ, is a New Testament way of proclaiming this radical renewal. It is not the donning of a costume any more than baptism is a mere cleansing of the body. But it is the sloughing off of worldly ways of thinking and acting, and then reproducing Christ's life in our own. Although our unique personalities remain, our deeper identities undergo transformation: "It is no longer I who live, but Christ who lives in me; and the life I now live in the flesh I live by faith in the Son of God, who loved me and gave himself for me" (Gal 2:20). The more Christ is our life, the more we become our true selves.

People spend so much time and money imitating celebrities, fashion models, actors, athletes, almost any high-profile individual who makes waves. Yet we don't become any more authentic by copying someone else's looks, attitude, style, and so forth. Rather, true personality gets occluded. With Christ, it is entirely different. All that is best and truest about a person is in him, and he communicates that to us by his grace, giving us a share in his divinity at the same time.

This is no small change. Just as it has for every disciple of every time and place, it will always require embracing the unknown, pushing off from the shore and into the deep, even though it feels more comfortable and secure to stay moored to the dock. Light is sometimes that unfamiliar element, compelling us to confront ourselves, to open our lives into a new direction, and to see what the Lord can do with our trusting surrender. What he will do is guaranteed to be uncomfortable, stretching us beyond our "presets," our predetermined capacities and resources.

If we are still bunkered down in darkness, we might be unknowingly resisting our own renewal—somewhat like the Jerusalem of our Lord's day, about which he tearfully complained: "Would that even today you knew the things that make for peace! But now they are hid from your eyes" (Lk 19:42).

And opening our eyes is exactly what Jesus wants to do. Just think of how ready the burdened and embattled people of Isaiah's prophecy would be for relief—but at the same time, not holding out much hope for redemption. Monotonous suffering always gives the threatening sense of sticking around forever—when one has been sick for a long spell, the feeling of health is a barely retrievable sensation. Hoping for better might seem like a waste of energy.

Opening our eyes to the light of Christ in our lives is really an opening of the heart to hope, to all that Jesus can do in our lives. Remember St. Thomas Aquinas: we move forward when we *hope* to find light. Without hope, without light, there is no point going in any direction. Hope might be the biggest step someone ever takes. For those immersed too long in darkness, choosing between surrendering to the undertow of helplessness and grabbing a lifeline can actually be a momentous decision. Too often, we opt for the path of least resistance, even if it is a downward one, instead of whatever effort it takes to turn our face to the sun. Didn't our Lord encounter unbelievable opposition from those who "loved darkness rather than light, because their deeds were evil" (Jn 3:19)?

The great light of Isaiah that pierced the darkness is indeed only fearsome to those bent on evildoing. Greater than sunlight or firelight, outshining the brightest lights generated by human technology, this ray is the response to the psalmist's cry, "Oh send out thy light and thy truth; let them lead me" (Ps 43:3). It is the light that alone can enlighten everyone born into this world. Coming directly from the "unapproachable light" of God, this is "Christ Jesus our hope," the Light of the World (see Jn 1:9; 1 Tim 1:1; 6:16).

He doesn't so much brighten up a dark room as help us look beyond the low ceiling of this world, help us see beyond the confines of our existence, whatever those confines might be. We must try to identify the forces in our lives that limit or frustrate us, the sins that continue to dog our progress, and ask ourselves whether we've really let the Lord into it. If we can't imagine a way out or through, if we can't picture what freedom and peace would look like for us, have we practically started to assume that God doesn't see any clearer than we do? Do we trust so much in our powers of analysis that we won't entertain solutions that only God can see?

When confronted with difficult choices and seemingly impossible obstacles, I often think of how St. Josemaría Escrivá would entrust all of his concerns to Our Lady by invoking a simple, but powerful, line from the "*Ave Maris Stella*," an ancient Marian hymn: "*Para iter tutum*," i.e., "prepare a safe path." I imagine Our Lady seeing all of the possibilities that we do not and cannot see; by our willingness to trust in her guidance, she then shows us the right path through the problem. This does not mean an *easy* path through the obstacle, but certainly the one God intends us to take.

It is here that our feelings of futility play us false. Humanly speaking, we have more than enough reasons to quit when progress appears stalemated. But if we truly believe that God sees not as man sees, and that the whole host of heaven sees all things in God, then we cannot afford to restrict ourselves to the confines of our imagination, judging impossible that which is only difficult or beyond our normal range of thought.

Therapists report that, in treating certain emotional disorders in clinical settings, some patients act on the assumption that the more intensely they feel something, the truer it is. The intensity of our feelings, in other words, is enough to persuade us that our perceptions are true. This is especially the case in treating debilitating fear and anxiety, where feelings are nothing if not persuasive. But feelings only reflect our perception of reality; they don't make reality to be what it is. Our perception may be clear or clouded, but whether we judge something good or bad, safe or unsafe, pleasant or painful, and so forth, our feelings will follow suit. Feelings correspond to our judgments.

The same is true of our spiritual state. In a sense, we get what we hope for. If we color everything black, we've effectively painted over every crack and crevice that could let in daylight. We might feel as though all options are exhausted, every effort futile, all ways blocked, and so be prepared to receive nothing from God. The parable of the talents makes this point, tapping into our human tendency to compare our share to others and resent the portion given us by the Lord. The servant who received least resented the small amount and did nothing with it. The others who received greater, though not equal, amounts traded and profited with them. And then comes the counterintuitive lesson: "I tell you, that to every one who has will more be given; but from him who has not, even what he has will be taken away" (Lk 19:26). God loves daring. God blesses audacious hope.

"A believer," writes St. John Climacus, "is not one who thinks that God can do everything, but one who believes that he will obtain all things."[2] It is one thing to acknowledge the theoretical power of a Supreme Being. If God is God, he must know all things and be capable of all things. Both our reason and the Bible tell us so. But to *so believe* in God that we trust that he is *personally* all-powerful and all-knowing even in our unremarkable, mundane lives, this shows a faith that has learned to walk on its own two feet.

Our hands were made by the Lord to both give and receive gifts, and we must firmly believe that he is not indifferent as to whether or not we do either one. God is not apathetic to the happenings of our lives. In the words of Romano Guardini, God "did not create the world and human race for men to play about in it like children on a heap of sand, not caring what they make of it so long as they behave themselves."[3]

God is not only adept at breaking into our self-made nightscape, he's also used to making something out of nothing, beginning with the cosmos, down to you and me. St. Augustine summarizes the grounds for his hope in terms of Christ's love for him, and condenses all of salvation history into a divine quest for us:

> At first, I was nothing, and He made me; I had been lost, and He sought me out; seeking me, He found me; when I was captive, He redeemed me; having

2   John Climacus, *The Ladder of Divine Ascent*, trans. Archimandrite Lazarus Moore (New York: Harper & Brothers, 1959), 117.

3   Romano Guardini, *The Living God* (New York: Pantheon Books, 1957), 67.

purchased me, He freed me; from being a slave, He made me His brother.[4]

The one who started out as nothing could have hardly imagined he would end up a brother to the Son of God, but hope kept adding links to this beautiful chain of graces. To feel like nothing, like a zero, seems pretty real to us. To feel trapped, captive, and enslaved can feel like a fact. But no condition is so desperate as to be beyond the Lord's field of vision, beyond the reach of his touch. Where there is nothing but our poverty and need, God provides:

> When the poor and needy seek water,
>> and there is none,
>> and their tongue is parched with thirst,
> I the Lord will answer them,
>> I the God of Israel will not forsake them.
> I will open rivers on the bare heights,
>> and fountains in the midst of the valleys;
> I will make the wilderness a pool of water,
> and the dry land springs of water. (Is 41:17–18)

The reality we had despaired of, our lifeless reality, suddenly comes alive with water and greenery. This is not to claim that God owes us miracles on demand. The point here is simply the point of prayer and spirituality in general:

4 Augustine of Hippo, Sermon 254, in *Sermons on the Liturgical Seasons*, trans. Sr. Mary Sarah Muldowney, RSM (New York: Fathers of the Church, Inc., 1959),347.

to unite ourselves to the will of God by opening ourselves to his ways, which are as far removed from ours as the heavens from the earth. Unreachable, unknowable are his ways unless he bends down to us and finds open ears to speak into. Hope opens our ears. Hope opens our eyes. Hope opens our hearts.

CHAPTER THREE
No Way Out?

Inwardly and outwardly man wrestles with his human limitations, only to
learn in the end that they are the means of his liberation.

—HUBERT VAN ZELLER[1]

ut is this hope, the hope that ended our last chapter, real? Nothing disappoints more than misplaced hope. And maybe nothing is easier to misplace than our hope. In a matter as critical as emerging from darkness, we need assurance that our hope for light is not an alluring mirage. Just as Jesus needed to reassure the quaking apostles that he was real after the Resurrection, ("Handle me, and see; for a spirit has not flesh and bones as you see that I have" [Lk 24:39]), so we need some assurance that our hope is more than a phantom.

Examples of human perseverance and payoff do not suffice here because our focus is not the short-term fulfillments that

1   Hubert van Zeller, *The Inner Search* (New York: Sheed and Ward, 1957), 7–8.

keep us trudging ahead through life. Satisfaction at reaching a goal is only right. But we are dealing with a transformation whose earmarks defy badge-earning, whose progress follows a way of surrender to ways above human ken. And thus to shore up our sense of hope in God, we must go to where God openly defies the worst human despair and frustration. The full tomb and the empty stomach, death and hunger, are two places in which the gospel situates the hopeless, and we will see in this chapter how God handily disposes of both.

Lazarus and the loaves, the dead man and the quasi-famine in the wilderness, let these stand for what hope in God can do for you. The resuscitation of a corpse and the superabundance of bread, however, should not create expectations of the selfsame results in our lives. While not excluding the miraculous, we yet need to get it into our hearts that where we see no way, God sees what we do not. And that, therefore, throwing up our hands in despair is really a self-defeating, self-imposed limitation on God's power and our ability to cooperate with him in faith. Has there ever been a saint who didn't do this and didn't feel the tension that accompanies such trust? Thus, in hoping, we should expect something along the lines of St. Paul's paradoxical "in hope he believed against hope" description of Abraham (Rom 4:18). There will be for us, in other words, a straining toward what we have not, as we endure the emptiness hope requires, awaiting divine fulfillment in God's time and way.

Jesus says, through the mouth of Abraham in a parable, that those who do not believe the promise of the Scriptures will likewise not be persuaded should someone rise from the dead (see Lk 16:19–31). People in the Gospels who have been dead (literally) or in lesser straits do indeed find new life at the word of Jesus, but it is only when received with faith and trust. Whether we will rise and walk or stay down for the count depends on our level of trust.

As St. Josemaría comments on the raising of Lazarus, our first Gospel example:

> Lazarus rose because he heard the voice of God and immediately wanted to get out of the situation he was in. If he hadn't *wanted to move, he would just have died again.*[2]
>
> Jesus is your friend. The Friend. With a human heart, like yours. With loving eyes that wept for Lazarus. And he loves you as much as he loved Lazarus. [...] Never despair. Lazarus was dead and decaying: "By now he will smell; this is the fourth day," says Martha to Jesus. If you hear God's inspiration and follow it—"Lazarus, come out!"—you will return to Life.[3]

That God sees what we don't see is no surprise. But how he makes us see what he alone is privy to almost always involves—more than mere surprise—a blindsided hit full of terror and wonder. And so we will begin in the darkest

[2] Escrivá, *The Forge*, 211.

[3] Josemaría Escrivá, *The Way* (New York: Scepter, 2002), 422, 719.

place on earth, the tomb, that we might absorb the full force of divine power. Beginning graveside, even witnessing the Son of God in tears, needs to be the bedrock of our hope in God's desire to lift us from the depths of our worst darkness. There is a way out, even from the tomb. If there isn't, then as St. Paul says, our faith is utterly in vain (see 1 Cor 15:12–19). This book, too, would be completely useless.

Recalled to Life: The Raising of Lazarus (Jn 11:1–44)

If we want to walk with a God who calls himself *resurrection* and *life*, we have to be ready for this question: "I am the resurrection and the life; he who believes in me, though he die, yet shall he live, and whoever lives and believes in me shall never die. Do you believe this?'" (Jn 11:25–26). We must think about our willingness to keep pace with this Lord who calls himself *resurrection* and *life* as we set the desperate scene of the miracle—even better to read the raising of Lazarus passage in full before further reflection.

Before our Lord arrives at this scene of mourning and distress, he had allowed everything to get as bad as it could possibly have gotten. Lazarus had taken ill and died. His corpse, having been anointed with aromatic spices and oils, was wrapped in a shroud and laid to rest in a tomb, which was sealed over by a heavy stone. It was all over.

All of this is an accomplished fact before the Lord even arrives—a full four days later. Many people have gathered to comfort the grieving sisters, Martha and Mary. The commotion of tragedy fills their house in Bethany. Then, and only then, does the Lord arrive. This is very much unlike other times in the Gospels, such as when the Lord filled St. Peter's fishing boats with a miraculous catch of fish that *almost* sank them, or when Jesus *almost* allowed another boat carrying the apostles to sink in a bad storm while he remained asleep in the stern—unlike those times, this time, there is no *almost*.

"Lazarus is dead," the Lord tells his disciples, adding, "For your sake, I am glad I was not there." This is God going totally contrary to everything that makes sense to human beings. We often think, "Lord, if you can, you should." He says, "Whoever lives and believes in me shall never die. Do you believe this?" If we want to walk with a God like this, I repeat, we have to be ready for this question. And this question not only opens the grave of Lazarus, it also unlocks the lesson of the miracle for us.

There are times when all seems lost, when all of our options are exhausted, when it even appears we have been forgotten by God. Sometimes the Lord allows things to get to a point where we are terrified, as the apostles were in a sinking boat; then suddenly things change, and there is calm. But not always. At other times, the Lord asks us to accept the fact that something is at an end and will not change, and to find our peace, our calm, in that.

The lesson of the raising of Lazarus is not that Jesus will always intervene in such extraordinary ways in our lives.

Those who are in the tombs will likely remain there. Most of the blind and crippled must remain so. What is even more important than extraordinary interventions is the ordinary ability to stand up. To stand up after repeated failures and after experiencing life's devastating moments shows that we are headed toward a final rising, an ultimate resurrection, after which there will be no further danger of falling, and every tear will be wiped away.

Jesus has permitted absolutely everything in our lives so that we will begin to see that there is only one way out. He allowed Lazarus to die. He allowed his sisters and neighbors to mourn. They had wrapped him in burial cloths, sealed the tomb, and never thought they would see him again in this world. Everything was said and done. Everyone, including Martha and Mary, knows that it's all over. And the only thing left to do is to weep, mourn, and console one another.

And then Jesus arrived. And there was no hope—regret, certainly, but no hope: "Lord, if you had been here," Martha says, "my brother would not have died" (Jn 11:21). "If you had been here…" *but you were not, and now there is nothing you can do.* How many times has a version of Martha's confusion escaped our lips? *Lord, if you had prevented me from doing this or that, or prevented something from happening, I would be better off today.* St. John Henry Newman says that this is one reason why Jesus wept: He was surrounded by that age-old question of man to his God: Why? Sometimes it is asked in faith, sometimes not, but it is always asked.[4]

We know that God is all love and all powerful. If he acts or does not act in our lives as we would expect, then his love and power are accomplishing something else, and always something greater. The raising of Lazarus is only a foreshadowing of the resurrection awaiting all who put their trust in the Lord. And that trust is often asked of us as we ourselves stand outside a tomb, experience the aftermath of tragedy or even suffer the consequences of our own failures.

The measure of what Christ can do in our lives depends upon our faith in him. We are told in the Gospels that on more than one occasion Jesus did not perform miracles because of a lack of faith. The raising of Lazarus was momentarily delayed by Martha's resistance. Jesus commanded, "Take away the stone," but on the pretext of a bad smell she prevented Him: "Lord, by this time there will be an odor, for he has been dead four days" (Jn 11:39). Implying what? *Lord, maybe this is beyond you. We have seen you heal the sick and do many other marvelous deeds, but… it has been four days*. Jesus said to her, "Did I not tell you that if you would believe you would see the glory of God?" (Jn 11:40). *Take away the stone!* He is indignant.

Do we believe that the Lord can do all things, and if he doesn't meet our expectations in life, that he has even better plans for us? "He who believes in me, though he die, yet shall

4   *Parochial and Plain Sermons*, Volume 3, Sermon 10: "Tears of Christ at the Grave of Lazarus."

he live. Do you believe this?" That is an open question, and it is our question. But always remember: in a place where all seems lost, the sound of Jesus' voice finds us, the tenderness of his compassion reaches us—and with a power that makes us rise up and return to life. He awakens us to new hope, whose final fulfillment is life without end.

How Much Do You Have? (Mk 6:35–44; Jn 6:1–13)

The Lord's multiplication of the loaves and fishes is another example of spent human reserves and resignation to failure. In this familiar story, pooled human resources yield scant provisions: five loaves and two fish. What to do? There is no way out for the apostles. And the people, thousands of them, are waiting. Jesus orders them all to sit in orderly fashion on the green grass and proceeds to feed one and all through the hands of the apostles.

But what preceded the order? A question. Jesus had asked, "How are we to buy bread, so that these people may eat?" (Jn 6:5). He asked this not because he was taken by surprise, nor because he was just thinking out loud, or hadn't planned ahead for this unforeseen crisis, but *to test them*. Whenever God asks a question, we have to be very careful. He already knows the answer. He's not looking for information. We know that he knows and he knows that he knows. But he puts us on the spot to draw something out of us that we may not know is there.

The Lord even says, "Go and see how many loaves you have" (Mk 6:38). The Lord wants this information from the apostles because it will reinforce the truth *to them* that they do not have enough to meet the need. He wants them to be crystal clear about that. A *pro forma* inventory follows and then the verdict: *We have only so many loaves and fish; what are they among so many?* Right. And we know what happens next. The Lord provides, but only after the apostles had admitted that they were outmatched by these circumstances.

Sometimes what comes out of us in a time of trial is anything but hope in the Lord. But as a part of our new life, he trains us to start thinking and believing in that way. Instead of panicking, Jesus wants us to learn that he knows—he sees us, he hears us, and with him we can do all things. "With God nothing will be impossible" (Lk 1:37) is not a slogan or a motto; it is eternal truth. And sometimes it takes multiple tests before we not only have the right answer on our lips, but that answer has also taken root in our hearts as *certitude*. As Job said, "I know that my Redeemer lives" (Jb 19:25). How could he be so sure? Because he had been through tests that would break any man, and he came through it without losing trust in God. He learned trust through what he suffered.

What circumstances are outmatching us right now? And what response is coming out of us? Is it hope?

Questions and tests from God come in many different ways,

from many sources, at odd times, and in strange places. When we hit an unexpected obstacle in our lives or continue to face an ongoing dilemma, we really have to see our Lord turning to us and asking: *How are we going to handle this? What is the solution?* And we should answer with the confidence of *knowing that he knows* and *knowing that he knows that he knows*. The Book of Sirach contains this powerful verse which should persuade us of his all-knowing gaze: "the eyes of the Lord are ten thousand times brighter than the sun; they look upon all the ways of men, and perceive even the hidden places" (Sir 23:19).

Nor should we forget that Jesus, even at his birth, enters the world in the quintessential dark place of the earth, the subterranean cave at Bethlehem, a powerful symbol of Christ's entrance into the hidden places of the human heart. Anyone who has descended the well-worn and narrow steps to the Grotto of the Nativity in Bethlehem will appreciate G. K. Chesterton's reflection that

> Christ was not only born on the level of the world, but even lower than the world. The first act of the divine drama was enacted, not only on no stage set up above the sightseer, but on a dark and curtained stage sunken out of sight.[5]

Project that humble precedent thirty years into the future, and should it surprise anyone that Jesus would frequent the gatherings of sinners and tax collectors? That he would go

5   G. K. Chesterton, *The Everlasting Man* (London: Hodder & Stoughton, 1925), 200.

in search of us—the lost sheep, the blind, the crippled, the maimed, the sick: those who have nowhere to go even if they could go somewhere? The light shines in the darkness, searches every shadowy corner, beginning even below the earth in a place where no child should be born, ending in places where no respectable man of Jesus' day would be caught dead. He doesn't go after anyone for whom he has no hope. God does nothing in vain.

If he sees so brightly as to penetrate us right through, as Sirach says, it is not to shame and humiliate but to instill confidence that in our vulnerability we can approach the Lord as we are, confident of being received.

Where Does It All Begin?

In fact, a concluding reflection showing the Lord acting on this very principle is especially relevant here. Jesus goes to where the broken pieces are, the rupture, the wound, and quietly begins to work there. Jesus inaugurates his public ministry "to seek and save the lost" (Lk 19:10) in… Bethlehem? Jerusalem? No. Capernaum. Why there? St. Matthew sees such enormous significance in the geography of the inauguration that he even counts one of Isaiah's greatest prophecies as fulfilled upon Jesus' relocating from Nazareth to "Capernaum by the sea" (Mt 4:13).

Capernaum was a town couched between the ancient tribal territories of Zebulun and Naphtali. By the time Christ came into the world, the boundaries separating them had been long erased. A brief biblical overview will tell us why.

After the Israelites entered the land of Canaan under Joshua around 1200 BC, each of the twelve tribes was given a portion of land, a tribal territory. The territories of the tribes Zebulun and Naphtali were side by side in the region of Galilee, beside the Sea of Galilee. Fast forward about five hundred years: when the Israelites were conquered and sent into exile by the Assyrians, the first two tribes to be overrun and deported—never to be heard from again—were those of Zebulun and Naphtali (see 2 Kgs 15:29). Yet about them Isaiah boldly predicts:

> But there will be no gloom for her that was in anguish. In the former time he brought into contempt the land of Zebulun and the land of Naphtali, but in the latter time he will make glorious the way of the sea, the land beyond the Jordan, Galilee of the nations. (Is 9:1)

Enter Jesus, roughly seven hundred years later. In his prophecy, Isaiah indicates that when the Messiah comes, his mission to restore Israel would begin in the very place where the unity of the tribes of Israel had ended: *The land of Zebulun and the land of Naphtali.* And so when Jesus "went and dwelt in Capernaum [...] in the territory of Zeb'ulun and Naph'tali" (Mt 4:13), St. Matthew picks up on the very subtle fulfillment of Isaiah's seemingly impossible prophecy:

> "The land of Zebulun and the land of Naphtali, toward the sea, across the Jordan,

Galilee of the Gentiles—
the people who sat in darkness
have seen a great light,
and for those who sat in the region and shadow of death
light has dawned." (Mt 4:15–16)

People move around a lot, especially in California, where I'm from. Much of the time, convenience dictates the move: commuting to a new job, a new school, and so forth. Why does St. Matthew see so much importance in the fact that Jesus is apparently *only* changing his address from Nazareth to Capernaum—perhaps also as a matter of convenience? Because the Lord's redemptive mission begins where the unity of God's people had initially ruptured. This answer is enormously important for anyone who feels their life irreparably broken.

Where does our personal restoration begin?

Jesus comes to meet us in the place where we fell apart—in our wounds, our traumas, our sins. It is a region of shadows and darkness, where we have grown accustomed to the darkness, and maybe we're not expecting (much less asking) God to go there, where we don't want him or anyone to see us. Is there a place in our lives that fits this description? A place where we're reluctant to let the Lord shine a light? Is he permitted by our housing authority to take up residence there?

People who have dwelt too long in darkness no longer

know how to see, to stand up, or walk with their heads held high. Rather, they are bowed down in grief, racked with pain, tormented. If our environment is all shadows, then we need someone to take us by the hand and pull us up to light and life. Jesus meets us in that place—in the place where we fell, and got used to being fallen. And he begins our restoration there—doubtless where it humbles us, but also where it is most needed.

And just as relatively few knew the significance of Jesus commencing his preaching of the kingdom from this humble town by the sea, so we may need to take a second look into our inner darkness to see where the Lord might be creating a new way out. In places that were only a memory on the map, the Lord commences to preach, save, and heal. Can't we daringly hope that he will do the same in our own inner country? Or do we put it beyond him, like emptying a tomb or filling thousands of hungry people?

CHAPTER FOUR
Know Yourself

That Christ you see is not Jesus. It is only the pitiful image that your blurred eyes are able to form... — Purify yourself. Clarify your sight with humility and penance. Then... the pure light of Love will not be denied you. And you will have perfect vision. The image you see will be really his. his!

—ST. JOSEMARÍA ESCRIVÁ[1]

It is obvious that we cannot love what we do not know.[2] No one falls in love with an unknown quantity. You can't love God unless you know him; nor can you love another human being or even yourself unless *some* knowledge is there. Depth of love depends on depth of knowledge. In each instance of love, truth is essential: errors about God, self, or others lead to distortions in thought and

---

1   Escrivá, *The Way*, 212.

2   See Augustine of Hippo, *The Trinity*, in *The Fathers of the Church: A New Translation*, trans. Stephen McKenna, CSSR (Washington, D.C.: The Catholic University of America Press, 1963), Book 10, chap. 1–5.

love—we may love an exceedingly idealized image of someone or despise the skewed caricature we've set up.

St. Josemaría's insight demonstrates how badly sin distorts our vision. In his *Way of the Cross*, he further observes that "it is our wretchedness that impedes us now from contemplating Our Lord, and makes his figure appear dark and distorted."[3] The original sin of our first parents turned God into an adversary or a competitor against our best interests. As soon as that happens, trust erodes, and if we are willing to follow him at all, we walk not by faith, but with caution. We make him earn our trust again and again. It is as though we repeat Adam and Eve's flight among the protective trees, fearful of our vulnerability before God.

Many people do not believe in God, much less love him, because of a distorted image of him. Nor do many devout souls draw as close to the Lord as they otherwise could, owing likewise to some mistaken notion of who he is. Among both the devout and the alienated, we find images of God the angry authority figure, God the perpetually displeased, God the vengeful, ever looking to get back at us for something.

Certainly God is depicted as angry, displeased, and avenging in Scripture. Humankind has given him good reason to be! And yet, that is not his identity, who he is, or how he wants to be known primarily by us. I am always delighted by the phrase in the Armenian Divine Liturgy, also found

3   Josemaría Escrivá, *The Way of the Cross* (New York: Scepter, 2002), 42

in Byzantine liturgies, that God is "lover of mankind." It is a title, a boast, not without a tinge of surprise. That God actually loves people who can be so ungrateful, hardhearted, even malicious, is truly something to be marveled at. And it accounts for all of the more "negative" qualities attributed to him in the Scriptures: he is only angry with us to the extent that we depart from the path of righteousness, the path that leads to our ultimate happiness, that is, unending life with him.

Modern people are insecure. And out of a misguided effort to anchor the insecure, contemporary spiritual writings and homilies sometimes downplay the gravity of human sin. The laudable effort to preserve people from the vortex of despair sometimes results in silence about our personal and collective misery. But ignoring our sinfulness does no service to God's overflowing mercy. Following the example of the saints, we must combine the deep sense of personal unworthiness with a proportionally boundless confidence in God.

We cannot set aside self-knowledge and honest self-examination. The distortions, borne of sin, that blur our knowledge of God and self render our relationship with him less real, less authentic than it should be. Two people who fall in love with a false image of each other love only the superficial. It is only a matter of time before full disclosure reveals the real objects of their love. Afterward, will the reality conform to the perception? Even more importantly: Will the love endure?

We only know God to the extent that he reveals himself in the Bible and in our interior life of prayer, and it is fully sufficient to elicit our love and devotion. Self-knowledge, on the other hand, only comes through honest and humble searching, not to mention the observations of others. We have no *book of self* that explains us in handbook fashion to ourselves. God does not want us to have this at our fingertips. Nor, by the way, does he want only a material knowledge of himself through the Scriptures minus the heart's devotion. For more on that, see Jesus' confrontations with the Pharisees.

Since knowledge of self is often painful, occasionally surprising, and sometimes demoralizing, we need to look first to the Lord. We need to go to the Light of the World, as St. Josemaría says, when our vision is clouded by what we see. Falling in love with him opens the dark ways of our souls to a light that we no longer need to fear. Because the more we know ourselves under God's light, the more we can appreciate *whom he loves* in loving us. And the greater our knowledge of our unworthiness, the greater our appreciation of the freeing gratuity of his love.

This is crucial. God does not love an ideal version of us; he loves us as we are, where we are, right now. What often thwarts our growth in self-knowledge is the fear that what we see will be so off-putting that God will be displeased and ashamed of us and turn away in disgust. Rather, he turns toward what is broken and miserable, even disgusting, to love it back to wholeness.

This is why we find the saints plunging into themselves to reveal more of themselves to God—to know what God is loving in them and why he needs to love it back to health. The further they go into self, the further they journey into God. The Lord's role of "physician" to the morally sick in the Gospels makes the point: he wants to meet sinners in their misery, not to leave them miserable, but to pour out his mercy as balm upon their wounds.

This explains how someone like St. Francis of Assisi could ask the Lord in his famous "Prayer before the Crucifix,"[4] "Enlighten the darkness of my heart." The beloved saint takes his inner darkness for granted and simply asks for a lamp to light his way. Does it seem like an ironic, strange, or exaggerated petition for such an eminently holy man?

But he's not finished: "...and give me true faith, certain hope, and perfect charity, sense and knowledge." How would we react to someone telling us that we have darkness in our heart, lack sense, are ignorant, and prove deficient in love? Maybe we would take it as an insult. But likely as not, it would demand effort to entertain the comment, much less receive it as true.

Saints have no problem with self-accusation, acknowledging (even boasting of) their frailty and faultiness. They have a

4   Sometimes known as "Most High and Glorious God."

better sense of where they've journeyed, where they're going, and the mercy that makes the journey possible, as in St. Paul's summary of the Christian itinerary: "He has delivered us from the dominion of darkness and transferred us to the kingdom of his beloved Son" (Col 1:13). Or the "called [...] out of darkness into his marvelous light" of St. Peter (1 Pt 2:9). For the saints, this is more than a metaphor. It is a reality *felt* by holy people who recognize the great gift of their salvation.

Ven. Fulton J. Sheen, using the Last Supper as his context, explains why saints are like this:

> In the presence of Divinity, no one can be sure of his innocence, and everyone asked, "Is it I?" Every man is a mystery to himself, for he knows that within his heart there lie, coiled and dormant, serpents that at any moment would sting a neighbor with their poison, or even God. One of them could be sure that he was the traitor, and yet no one could be sure that he was not.[5]

This sense of uncertainty need not give way to insecurity. Rather, it summons from us a radical trust. Even if we were the unknowing guilty one, trust in the mercy of Christ would override even our betrayal, bringing us to our knees before him. Simon Peter had such a radical trust. It took several tremendous failures to get him there, but he could eventually accept the mysterious darkness within his heart that had blocked self-knowledge and distorted his sense of self. Lesson

5   Fulton J. Sheen, *Life of Christ* (New York: McGraw-Hill, 1958), 342–343.

learned, and a saint was made.

The nearer we are to God, the more we feel our feet are made of clay. And not just our feet. Everything about us seems to fluctuate, waver, and, like clay, be capable of morphing into one thing or another. Archbishop Sheen's words complement St. Francis' prayer: we don't see ourselves with perfect clarity. Blinders or filters, call them what you will, are the optical handicaps we are all born with. Many claims we make about ourselves, others, or life in general need to be hedged with disclaimers of shortsightedness. Here, the Lord's words are especially convicting:

> Jesus said, "For judgment I came into this world, that those who do not see may see, and that those who see may become blind." Some of the Pharisees near him heard this, and they said to him, "Are we also blind?" Jesus said to them, "If you were blind, you would have no guilt; but now that you say, 'We see,' your guilt remains." (Jn 9:39–41)

Those who claim sight are already on thin ice before God. Unless you have a prophet's anointing upon you, circumspection is indispensable when coming before the Lord. The parable of the Pharisee and the tax collector demonstrates this point (Lk 18:9–14). The one who stood in the temple thanking God for his righteousness was in reality exalting himself, blind all along to his own arrogance. But the tax collector who knew that he possessed no righteousness prayed accordingly and found justification: "God, be merciful to me a sinner!" (Lk 18:13). The former thought he saw; the latter thought nothing except that God is merciful.

Moreover, Fr. Merton wryly muses about whether any individuals actually exist who see reality as it truly is:

> I wonder if there are twenty men alive in the world now who see things as they really are. That would mean that there were twenty men who were free, who were not dominated or even influenced by any attachment to any created thing or to their own selves or to any gift of God, even to the highest, the most supernaturally pure of His graces. I don't believe that there are twenty such men alive in the world. But there must be one or two. They are the ones who are holding everything together and keeping the universe from falling apart.[6]

What most colors our perception, he suggests, is attachment. In the vocabulary of spirituality, attachment normally means an unhealthy or disordered clinging to someone or something outside of God. As soon as we attach ourselves, we cease to enjoy liberty of spirit, the full freedom of God's children, because we intend to depend on something else for meaning and happiness. As spiritual authors often point out, an attachment can be as slight as a string or as substantial as flesh and blood. The point is not so much *what it is* as the effect it has upon the soul. St. John of the Cross'

---

6   Thomas Merton, *New Seeds of Contemplation* (New York: New Directions, 1972), 203.

famous analogy is worth mentioning here:

> It makes little difference whether a bird is tied by a thin
> thread or by a cord. Even if it is tied by thread, the bird
> will be held bound just as surely as if it were tied by
> cord; that is, it will be impeded from flying as long as
> it does not break the thread. Admittedly the thread is
> easier to break, but no matter how easily this may be
> done, the bird will not fly away without first doing so.
> This is the lot of those who are attached to something:
> No matter how much virtue they have they will not
> reach the freedom of the divine union.[7]

Probably the most automatic attachment any of us has
is to our own point of view, the way we see things. How we
see ourselves, God, our spiritual and moral states, how we
view the world, these are the sticking points for most of us.
Which is no problem if what we believe is true, if our eyes are
clear of both beam and splinter. But since the scales usually
fall from our eyes only gradually, it is far better to keep a
loose grip on our opinions and perceptions. We should cling
tightly only to revealed truth and the authoritative teaching
of the Church. We can go wrong on many points, but not
on Creeds and Catechisms.

We, like the saints, need to see ourselves honestly. And this
begins with knowing, first, how God sees us. Scripture makes

---

7   John of the Cross, *The Ascent of Mount Carmel*, in *The Collected Works of St. John
    of the Cross*, trans. Kieran Kavanaugh, OCD, and Otilio Rodriguez, OCD
    (Washington, DC: ICS Publications, 1991), 1.11.4,p. 143.

no secret of the Lord's perspective: we are created very good, are even *wonderfully* made, and are certainly redeemable after sin. Even more, we are created to enjoy a nuptial, spousal union with God forever. As we allow these truths to penetrate mind and heart, we become aware of all that stands in the way of what God wants for us. Our inner disorder stands out—those obstacles we place before God's work in our souls—and we begin to want them all *out*. And because we know that we can't see everything about ourselves, we might just begin to ask the Lord to enlighten the darkness of our hearts, to give us true faith, certain hope, and perfect love.

If Archbishop Sheen's reflection above conveys a sense of ever teetering on the edge of betrayal and/or infidelity, that is not exactly the point. Rather, he places in high relief our utter dependence upon the grace of God for any good we do, any virtue we possess, any claim we can make to being disciples of Jesus. The saints are very sensitive to this reality, and they live and pray with corresponding trust. What might begin as discouragement and practical despair over our weakness becomes for the saint the strongest motive for trust in God.

St. Paul's excruciating inner struggle over disturbances in his flesh, combined with seemingly unheard prayers for relief, eventually erupted into praise and thanksgiving to the Lord for his power, and a humble boasting on the part of the apostle for being the occasion of such a display of divine strength:

Three times I besought the Lord about this, that it should leave me; but he said to me, "My grace is sufficient for you, for my power is made perfect in weakness." I will all the more gladly boast of my weaknesses, that the power of Christ may rest upon me. For the sake of Christ, then, I am content with weaknesses, insults, hardships, persecutions, and calamities; for when I am weak, then I am strong. (2 Cor 12:8–10)

He does a complete about-face from humiliating inner conflict to total surrender and complete trust. But St. Paul really needed to taste his own poverty before he was open to the lesson. Stumbling in the dark—especially in our self-made darkness—readies us to follow the first streaks of light that appear. The same is true of St. Peter. His brash claim at the Last Supper, "Though they all fall away because of you, I will never fall away" (Mt 26:33), was soon demolished by multiple denials of the Lord. He needed to fail in order to learn. Faced with the prospect of trials, none can presume strength and perseverance, none can rely on self: "Therefore let any one who thinks that he stands take heed lest he fall" (1 Cor 10:12).

Among devout people, there can be a desire to present a clean record to Jesus. We would like to be able to say that we have "never" done this or would "never" do that. But "never" is a two-edged sword. To "keep oneself unstained from the world" (Jas 1:27), is obviously pleasing to God and something to strive for. But not at the expense of trust. If our dependence on God diminishes even slightly, if our confidence in him starts getting edged out by self-reliance, the Lord may even allow us to fail on those very points where pride had started to gain ground. His purpose is not to shame and humiliate, but to bring us back into the reality and power of his grace. It is pure fiction to believe that we can attain any good on our own, and Jesus won't have his followers living in a fantasyland, worshipping a God who is impressed or placated by self-made men.

Keeping Up Appearances

Returning to the Upper Room, we find the question, "Is it I, Lord?" (Mt 26:22) on everyone's lips, yet one of them asks it just to keep up appearances. Judas is about to set up Jesus for arrest and condemnation. And the Lord knows every step Judas will take to the chief priests, every thought in his heart, every word he will speak in procuring a band of soldiers and finalizing the logistics of this night of treachery and capture. He knows the precision of the plan that will bring Judas and company into Gethsemane in the dead of night. And that terrible signal… Jesus knows Judas will draw within a breath of him, easing the way for a greeting kiss.

As the wheels of the Passion are set in motion, we think of the outrage Judas commits against the Lord. But if we think that a comparable betrayal would be unthinkable for us, then, as Archbishop Sheen says, we must think again. In words deliberately artless and blunt, St. Josemaría makes the selfsame point: "As long as I am on earth, I, too, am capable of doing something terribly stupid."[8] Here is a man, a saint like Francis, who has no desire to keep up appearances. His need is to be real—which does not mean sinful or complacent, but humble. The humility of a fallen person is the forthrightness to say without blinking not only that he is generally prone to sin, but fully capable of committing any and every sin. We may not be inclined to this or that sin, and may never do this or that evil thing, but the vicious roots are there.

As St. Josemaría attests:

When I feel capable of all the horrors and all the errors committed by the most wretched people, I understand well that I myself can be unfaithful... But this uncertainty is one of the bounties of God's Love, which leads me to hold tightly, like a child, to the arms of my Father, fighting every day a little so as not to separate myself from Him.[9]

Reminding us of our utter helplessness, God sometimes allows us to feel the sting, the allure of temptation, or to feel simple weakness of mind or body, so that we will cling "tightly, like a child" to him.

8   Josemaría Escrivá, *In Dialogue with the Lord* (New York: Scepter, 2018), 161.

9   Escrivá, *The Way of the Cross*, 91.

In the wake of temptation, we should be able to say, without being the least bit ironic: *I can be malicious, hypocritical, self-righteous, perverse, gross, and cruel.* That's you and that's me. I think if we don't see this about ourselves then our salvation won't mean as much to us as it should. After all, what is God saving us from? Just one or two really big sins? No, Jesus died to save us from *all* sins. And if we're not malicious or cruel, it is because he has stepped in our paths and prevented us. This was St. Thérèse of Lisieux's conviction, that if she had never committed a grave sin, it was owing to God's prevention rather than to her own moral strength.[10]

In declaring his waywardness, St. Gregory of Narek claimed that he had even discovered some new sins, unaccounted for since the time of Adam:

For you, [my miserable soul,] have indulged with unsparing excess

in the harvest of all the human evils

from Adam till the end of the species, and even found some new ones,

despised and repugnant to your creator, God.[11]

It is hard to hang our nametag on a sin, much less on *all* sins as St. Gregory does here. But in a saying that has become

10 *The Story of a Soul*, Chapter 4: First Communion and Confirmation.

11 Gregory of Narek, *Speaking with God from the Depths of the Heart: The Armenian Prayer Book of St. Gregory of Narek*, trans. Thomas J. Samuelian, 4th ed. (Yerevan, Armenia: Vem Press, 2015), prayer no. 9.

axiomatic among devotees of the Divine Mercy devotion, propagated through the writings of St. Faustina Kowalska, we find an unexpected incentive to confessing our faults and, especially, to trust: "The greater the sinner, the greater his right to [God's] mercy."[12] This is more or less an echo of Romans 5–6 where St. Paul is at pains both to establish and to celebrate the utter gratuity of God's grace:

> But the free gift is not like the trespass. For if many died through one man's trespass, much more have the grace of God and the free gift in the grace of that one man Jesus Christ abounded for many. (Rom 5:15)

And yet he is very quick to forestall those who might suggest that sinning freely would be the cause of yet more abundant grace. "By no means!" he exclaims (Rom 6:2). The point being made by St. Paul, St. Faustina, St. Gregory, St. Francis, and all other holy people, is that grace and mercy change us, and need to change us. But they can only change those who self-identify as "sick" people whom the Divine Physician came to heal—the Divine Physician who said in the same breath that he had not come "to call the righteous, but sinners to repentance" (Lk 5:31–32).

The depth of our need for Jesus cannot be adequately appreciated without a sincere, if uncomfortable, descent into the depths of self-knowledge. And this is to open wounds,

---

12 Faustina Kowalska, *Diary: Divine Mercy in My Soul* (Stockbridge, MA: Marian Press, 2005), no. 423.

to expose sicknesses of the soul. All of our unrighteousness, self-righteousness, secret sins, and self-indulgence, all of these must be manifested voluntarily before the eyes of him who sees us.

This sounds like we not only have to be in a bad place to know Christ's power, but to *know* that we are in a bad place. Many don't know their own misery. And I don't think any of us knows the full extent of our need for God, our dependence on his grace, and how much our salvation is his doing. In the Book of Revelation, the Lord excoriates those who say, "I am rich, I have prospered, and I need nothing," not knowing all the while that they are "wretched, pitiable, poor, blind, and naked" (Rev 3:17). And how naturally he counsels obtaining from him "salve to anoint your eyes, that you may see" (Rev 3:18).

If bad news is often given as an appetizer for the good, then exploring our inner darkness must precede our personal evangelization, just as it always will be for disciples of Jesus. If the keynote of his gospel preaching is "repent, and believe in the gospel" (Mk 1:15), then beyond doubt we must look inward first, even at the risk of being initially dismayed by what we see.

The purpose here is not to convince anyone of their rottenness, nor to pull the rug out from under anyone's hard-fought self-esteem, but to focus on what the gospel needs to address. If we were not fundamentally very good, our badness wouldn't make us feel like we're living in an unworthy way. As it is, we often have an inner sense of frustrated goodness, frustrated generosity, of falling short, of never really going beyond what's comfortable.

Jesus does not preach his saving message into a vacuum, into a world that has no pressing need for help. He does not evangelize those who have it all together and might just need a little fine-tuning. "It is not as if a good life of some sort came first," St. Augustine pointedly comments, "and that thereupon God showed his love and esteem for it from on high, saying: 'Let us come to the aid of these men and assist them quickly because they are living a good life.' No, our life was displeasing to him." He continues:

> We were not good, but God had pity on us and sent his Son to die, not for good men but for bad ones, not for the just but for the wicked. Yes, Christ died for the ungodly. [...] Yet although men's actions were [evil], God in his mercy did not abandon men. He sent his Son to redeem us, not with gold or silver but at the price of his blood poured out for us. Christ, the spotless lamb, became the sacrificial victim, led to the slaughter for the sheep that were blemished—if indeed one can say that they were blemished and not entirely corrupt. Such is the grace we have received! Let us live so as to be worthy of that great grace, and not do injury to it. So mighty is the physician who has come to us that he has healed all our sins! If we choose to be sick once again,

we will not only harm ourselves, but show ingratitude to the physician as well.[13]

That we could choose sickness over health is an alarming thought. And yet it is a very real possibility for any who have waged war against longstanding (and especially addictive) sin. Quoting Proverbs, St. Peter lays out an image—unpleasant but real—of what this looks like in nature: "The dog turns back to his own vomit, and the sow is washed only to wallow in the mire" (2 Pt 2:22). That we would willingly and repeatedly corrupt ourselves can be a sign of many things, including ingratitude, but in the end it is a demonstration of how much we are in need of the physician.

As painful as it is to come by, this self-knowledge is indispensable for spiritual and emotional growth; it is a path we may never abandon if we hope to attain glory with Christ in heaven. Fr. Theodossios-Marie of the Cross draws a straight line between our willingness to know the truth about ourselves and our share in the glory of the Lord:

To penetrate and deepen the mystery of the Transfiguration and any mystery whatsoever of Our Lord's life, wherever I am, with all my weaknesses, I must see myself and smile at the Lord who permits me to see myself. If I am not able to thank him for what he

13 Augustine, Sermon 23A, in *Liturgy of the Hours*, vol. 4, 1–4: CCL 41, 321–323, pp. 188–189.

allows me to see of my misery, then I cannot perceive that what he is showing me contains my resurrection and my transfiguration.[14]

The connection between our weakness, our misery, and our future glory ("my resurrection and my transfiguration") cannot be overemphasized. We often shun the recognition of our faultiness because we feel diminished and humiliated by it. No wonder: in a culture that so prizes image, personal appearance, power, and strength, we feel more than a little awkward rejoicing in our weaknesses. After all, isn't that what misfits do? Isn't it the pitiful attempt of losers to get attention at any cost?

But as St. Paul discovered in his thorn in the flesh, and as many other saints have likewise learned, human poverty, human wretchedness, is the Lord's inroad to our souls. More than a crack, it is a broad highway down which his grace and love can travel so as to transform us from self-reliant creatures into humble, joyful lovers. On a purely human level, we know how difficult it can be to live with people whose self-knowledge is scant and who resist going deeper into themselves. The opposite is also true: how comforting it is to live with the humble, those who laugh at themselves, easily apologize, and serve others with simplicity.

14 Theodossios-Marie of the Cross, *Discover the Other Universe: The Sacred Way of the Redemption* (Rome: Gracewing and Millenium Romae Editrice, 1998), 70–71.

Self-Knowledge and Discipleship

Knowing ourselves as best we can is crucial to another essential aspect of discipleship: denying ourselves and carrying our cross daily. It sounds paradoxical, but if the Lord Jesus asks us to deny ourselves daily, first we have to know who that self is whom we are denying. Otherwise, it seems to me, we might blindly try to embrace pain or curtail healthy and holy movements of our humanity, and not really deny what needs renunciation. The tendency of some unenlightened souls to give up any pleasure that comes their way, for example, often leads to a kind of scrupulosity that is far more detrimental to spiritual growth than the enjoyment of wholesome pleasures in their time.

The great Carmelite contemplative, St. Elizabeth of the Trinity, is very eloquent on this point. In line with many saints and mystics, she mentions very frequently the need to forget self. In her prayer to the most Holy Trinity, probably her best-known work, her first petition is precisely for self-forgetfulness. It is as though her relationship with God—her union with him and her spiritual growth—depends upon this as a first principle:

> O my God, Trinity whom I adore, help me to forget myself entirely that I may be established in You as still and as peaceful as if my soul were already in eternity. May nothing trouble my peace or make me leave You, O my Unchanging One.[15]

15 Elizabeth of the Trinity, "O My God, Trinity Whom I Adore," in *Elizabeth of the Trinity: The Complete Works*, vol. 1, trans. Sr. Aletheia Kane, OCD (Washington, DC: ICS Publications, 1984), 183.

Or quoting St. Paul, she writes:

"Walk in Jesus Christ," he tells me, "be rooted in Him, built up in Him, strengthened in faith, growing more and more in Him through thanksgiving." *To walk in Jesus Christ* seems to me to mean to leave self, lose sight of self, give up self, in order to enter more deeply into Him with every passing moment, so deeply that one is *rooted* there; and to every event, to every circumstance we can fling this beautiful challenge: "Who will separate me from the love of Jesus Christ?"[16]

Does it make sense why this is necessary? Behind it all is love's natural desire to surrender itself wholly to the beloved. It is not more complicated than that. How this plays out in the spiritual life might take some looking into, but in the best human love, surrender is the automatic response of lover to beloved. It is a denial of our wishes and preferences for the sake of uniting with and serving another. Although this takes different forms at different stages of a relationship, the reality remains the same. The self-denial may become subtler over time, more habitual, than at the beginning when emotions are stronger. And this simply reveals how love matures, how love refines over time. The more love develops into a virtuous habit, the more it becomes a way of life, the less it remains a generous impulse that activates only occasionally.

16 Elizabeth of the Trinity, 156–7.

As we grow in self-knowledge, it becomes increasingly clear what parts of self need to be told no. It becomes a practical matter of identifying what is getting in the way of our union with God and getting rid of those things that are hindering it. This progresses from eliminating serious sin and deliberate venial sin to cutting out other things that increasingly appear as incompatible with living a life of holiness, of deep prayer.

This is why in religious houses, monasteries, and convents, you find what are generally called "observances." Among those living the consecrated (or vowed) life, there are rules regulating silence, use of the media, meals, clothing, recreation, and many other departments of life—all of which are aimed at fostering each person's central relationship with God and harmonious living with one's brethren. The further we go in the spiritual life, the more sensitive we become to what promotes union with God and fraternal charity and what blocks them. The closer we are to God, the details of love become clearer. The more intimate the union, the less we want to be tripping over self.

If someone reacts against the idea of leaving or denying self, it might be the residual effect of living in a culture where everyone seems to be struggling with self-worth, where many record all the events of their lives on social media, where commercial advertising is so pervasive, where "likes," "shares," and "followers" are valued as crucial validators, the measure of one's overall worth.

How can we leave behind someone who needs affirmation, who is still half-formed, who is still searching for identity? We cannot forget something we never knew in the first place. We cannot leave behind what we have never found. Sometimes people will set up self-esteem as the chief obstacle in their spiritual growth, when it really isn't the proper focus. They feel inadequate much of the time—as though everyone around them somehow "has it all together," everyone except them. No one "has it all together," whatever that actually means. Jesus is Savior of those who *don't* have it all together. I shouldn't mind that I don't have it all together. What should bother me is if I don't trust him in whom all things, in heaven and on earth, come together.

If I don't fix my gaze on Christ to uncover the truth about myself, then inevitably I will look to all of those shallow qualities that the world so highly values. To be happy and at peace, I will need others to like me, approve of me, agree with me, and so on. But the happiness and peace generated will have very short lifespans and leave me lower than when I began. When you build on an unsubstantial foundation, the structure will fall with the first contrary wind.

We often need others to help us see our basic goodness, to hold up a mirror to us. Yet even if we lack this affirmation, the Lord can supply for it. Indeed, all true affirmation of our goodness must be rooted in the truth about who God has made us to be, which is living likenesses of himself. Even if the image has been distorted or shattered through sin, the Lord knows how all the broken pieces fit together. He can not only restore us, but by grace make us into something greater, into himself.

CHAPTER FIVE
A Most Vehement Flame

Love is strong as death, jealousy is cruel as the grave. Its flashes are flashes
of fire, a most vehement flame.

—SONG OF SONGS 8:6

burning lamp is a biblical symbol of vigilance, fidelity. Waiting servants, no less than the ten virgins of the wedding party, are expected to keep their lamps supplied with oil for one obvious purpose: keeping the flame lit. Less the oil, the clay vessel sits like a dead battery, useless. But even more: the heart devoid of the oil of love likewise sits as a cold, blackened shell, waiting to be filled by something. It is not a difficult leap from the symbol to the reality of fidelity in waiting. If the lamp's flame means more than light to see by, so the love it signifies means more than a temporary warmth of affection. Love that remains constant and strong, no matter how long you have to wait for its consummation, is the gospel demand.

It is no surprise that the Lord needs to exhort us to this vigilance. In the Lord's absence, as in the absence of anyone whom we want to impress, we put our feet up. Waiting creates tension, and everyone wants relief from the pull between expectation and fulfillment. Hence, Jesus' parables urgently remind us that love tends to slacken in the prolonged absence of the beloved. Formerly diligent servants begin eating and drinking to excess, mistreating their fellow servants, and so get caught scrambling when the Master comes (see Mt 24:45–51). In waiting for the Lord is the trial of love and fidelity.

Is this an unforeseen and unfortunate test? No, says St. John Henry Newman. Vigilance, he observes, is a distinctively Christian virtue. He imaginatively compares Christian spiritual instincts to the natural instincts of animals who often sense what humans cannot readily perceive. Just so, he says, Christians have a hidden but real *sense* for the presence and activity of Christ in their lives, which those without an active faith and hope fail to perceive. Christians look out for Christ, hope for him, and love him whenever they encounter him.

> They, then, watch and wait for their Lord, who are tender and sensitive in their devotion towards Him; who feed on the thought of Him, hang on His words; live in His smile, and thrive and grow under His hand. They are eager for His approval, quick in catching His meaning, jealous of his honour. They see Him in all

things, expect Him in all events, and amid all the cares, the interests, and the pursuits of this life, still would feel an awful joy, not a disappointment, did they hear that He was on the point of coming.[1]

From watching and waiting, a properly Christian love emerges. As Christ loved his own unto the end (see Jn 13:1), so our own persevering love mirrors his as we love God and neighbor unwaveringly throughout life.

Combining the two images of light and love, St. Thérèse of Lisieux memorably applies the Lord's words in the Sermon on the Mount to our need to love consistently on all fronts:

> Charity must not remain hidden in the bottom of the heart. Jesus has said: *"No one lights a lamp and puts it under a bushel basket, but upon the lampstand, so as to give light to ALL in the house."* It seems to me that this lamp represents charity which must enlighten and rejoice not only those who are dearest to us but "ALL *who are in the house*" without distinction.[2]

Selective charity signals spiritual atrophy. Love refused to anyone cramps the soul of the disciple, and prayer no longer takes flight. When animosity or resentment weigh us down, especially during prayer time, our thoughts and feelings

1   John Henry Newman, "Waiting for Christ," in *Sermons Preached on Various Occasions* (London: Longmans, Green, and Co., 1908), 35.

2   Thérèse of Lisieux, *Story of a Soul*, trans. John Clarke, OCD (Washington, D.C.: ICS, 1996), 220.

turn toxic as we stew over the causes of our discontent. Once prayer becomes mainly thinking or "processing," it ceases to accomplish its purposes of offering worship to God and expanding our hearts to become like his.

In beginning a relationship, or even an engaging project, sustaining enthusiasm takes no effort. But as time passes and tangible rewards diminish, love may lose its focus and fall to seeking distractions and entertainment where once it couldn't take its eyes off of the beloved person or object. And not infrequently, when we feel fatigued or unrewarded by the routine of our lives, we fall back on statistics: how much time we've spent doing one thing or another, the miles we've gone, whether someone has told us thank you or not. *Somehow*, we think, *all these things should be adding up. I should see and feel the difference that all of this is making.*

Would things change if we were to know that God is perfectly vigilant over us? Pursuing us, in fact, all the time? Would we live with greater intensity of purpose, with eyes and ears ever open to him, if we could appreciate that Christ runs to us, "crying out by words, by deeds, by death, by life, by descending, by ascending—crying out that we must return to Him"?[3] If we seem to be the ones doing all the work to make ourselves happy, to keep our lives livable and

---

3 Augustine of Hippo, *Confessions*, in *The Fathers of the Church: A New Translation*, trans. Vernon J. Bourke (Washington, DC: The Catholic University of America Press, 1953), Book IV, ch. 12, pp 89–90.

fulfilling, the Gospels provide an alternative narrative—indeed, all of salvation history tells an altogether different story, the true one:

At every time and in every place, God draws close to man. He calls man to seek him, to know him, to love him with all his strength. He calls together all men, scattered and divided by sin, into the unity of his family, the Church. To accomplish this, when the fullness of time had come, God sent his Son as Redeemer and Savior.[4]

As the *Catechism of the Catholic Church* beautifully notes, God's closeness to us is more than an idea. It takes flesh in Christ. When he became man and began walking the earth, he did not go about aimlessly. He went in pursuit of sinners. The Son follows our tracks into whatever caves, dens, or pits we have retreated into to protect the meager happiness we've cobbled together for ourselves. When he finds us he questions our success, "Well, my friend, is it working? Have you found happiness all on your own? How long do you think it will last?"

Jesus takes our happiness very seriously. But the first thing we need to know about happiness is what it is not. Human happiness is something very specific, rooted not in the flesh but in the spirit. It is communion with God

4   Catechism of the Catholic Church, 2nd ed. (Washington, DC: Libreria Editrice Vaticana–United States Conference of Catholic Bishops, 2000), 1.

in the greatest possible intimacy forever—without fear of loss or corruption of the relationship. We are penetrated and filled completely with the infinite love for which God created us. That is heaven. Forever. Hell is the absence of all of that, also forever.

In one of his most powerful sermons, St. Augustine exposes the truly infinite chasm between our limited designs for happiness and the beatitude were born for. He depicts God showing up in our midst and giving us carte blanche to do anything we crave, however indulgent or violent—and moreover, all may be done without the slightest qualm of conscience, and be enjoyed endlessly. But there's a catch.

> I am going to ask you a question, but it is one that you must put to yourselves. Suppose God came and spoke to us here in his own voice. [...] Imagine that he is here and saying to one of you, "Do you want to sin? All right, go ahead, then: sin. Do anything that gives you pleasure. Anything that you love on earth shall be yours. You are angry with someone? Fine: let him die. You want to lay violent hands on someone? He is yours to seize. If you want to hit someone, you can hit him. If you want someone condemned, condemned he shall be. Whatever you want for yourself, you shall possess it. No one is to oppose you, no one is to say to you, 'What are you doing?' No one will say to you, 'Don't do that.' No one will say, 'Why did you do it?' All the earthly things you crave shall be yours in

abundance. You shall live to enjoy them not just for a time but always. But there is just one reservation: you will never see my face."[5]

Immediately, a reaction rumbled through the congregation; the people must have groaned quite audibly because, in the next line of the text, St. Augustine asks, "You groaned when I said that, my brothers and sisters. Why did you groan?" Or we might ask ourselves, if we *did not* groan, *why didn't we?* It's hard to read St. Augustine's words impassively, and we should feel relieved if we winced at the end. Even if our ideas of happiness are limited—and sometimes plain wrong—we've at least got some intuition that doing whatever pleases us endlessly is not the answer. Something about seeing God's face completes us. And something about waiting faithfully for that vision changes us in ways truly preparatory for the sight. If only the pure of heart see God, how intensely vigilant must we be to make sure our desires are singly focused and not scattered over a host of amusements and sense pleasures.

What causes burnout among servants of God is very often seeking something less than God as our happiness. In waiting for him, it is not so much that our flame goes out, but rather that it searches for other things to burn, to consume. The restless servants of the Lord's parable begin to consume food

5 Augustine of Hippo, "Exposition of Psalm 127," *The Works of Saint Augustine: A Translation for the 21st Century*, Part III, Vol. 6, *Expositions of the Psalms: 121–150*, trans. and notes Maria Boulding, OSB, ed. Boniface Ramsey,(Hyde Park, New York: New City Press, 2016), section 9, pp. 112–3.

and drink to excess, to get drunk and even abuse their fellow servants. When we stop refilling our lamp with the vital oil it needs to keep our flame alight, the burning turns destructive. We consume whatever is at hand, however dangerous to our spiritual and physical wellbeing. This helps us better understand why the Lord is so proactive about our happiness and so eager to orient us firmly in the right direction. This is also why God becomes man: to meet us where we stray. God goes where we least expect him in order to show us the way out.

Jesus asks, as though it should be common sense for us, "What man of you, having a hundred sheep, if he has lost one of them, does not leave the ninety-nine in the wilderness, and go after the one which is lost, until he finds it?" (Lk 15:4). We search frantically for a lot of relatively unimportant things that we nevertheless take very seriously. Looking all over for car keys, cell phone, or something as small as a paperclip—each useful and even necessary in its own way—but possessing nothing like the importance of one human soul.

Well, whatever examples you wish: sheep, cell, car keys— the Lord implies, if I may say, *you get the point*. He's always got his eyes on us. And when he steps into the trenches of human misery, he reaches out to those whom he generally identifies as "the sick" (Mt 9:12). The sick can neither heal themselves, nor move themselves to higher ground, nor sometimes even identify their own illness. This may be especially true when the symptoms are not patently the result of sin, but a general feeling of dissatisfaction or frustration. When the cause of our spiritual lethargy is not easily identifiable as this or that sin, rising up from one's languor is not an obvious step up a ladder.

As mentioned earlier, healing for our sickness always comes from a deep encounter with the living God: *as we are*, not as we would like to be. It is not, *Once I've gotten my act together, gotten sober, become virtuous—then I'll start being "religious."* No, it's in the sickness itself that the Divine Physician seeks to join up with us, to share our food and our conversation, to heal us. God goes out to meet the Prodigal Son, rests at a well to meet a jaded woman, and sits at table with tax collectors and sinners in St. Matthew's house. The bond created as the Lord descends into our worst states is the relationship that saves us: between Savior and sinner, between Physician and the sick.

Staying with these three persons from the Gospels for a moment, we see combined both moral failure and a general sense of burnout. The Samaritan woman who came out to draw water in the heat of the day (Jn 4:1–42), the Prodigal Son impatiently asking for his inheritance (Lk 15:11–32), St. Matthew sitting at his tax office (Lk 5:27–32): all are sick of what they've got, even if they possess a lot—a series of paramours, an inheritance, a sizeable cut of tax money. Money, freedom, lovers, things that so many people fall for as equaling happiness: each leads inevitably to boredom and regret.

Burnout is inevitable, however great the accumulation of wealth and pleasure, as St. Josemaría implies:

> That is why you find so many people who from a human point of view ought to be ever so happy, yet they go about uneasy and embittered. They appear to be overflowing with happiness, but just scratch beneath the surface of their souls and you will discover a bitterness more bitter than gall.[6]

Deep Desires of the Soul

Forcing this world's goods to supply for the deep desires of the soul is demanding the impossible. As everything begins to become stale or corrupted, the protagonist in all the gaining is drained. The burned-out might pray out of sheer exhaustion, "Lord, make my life a little easier. Lord, make my life a little more ideal." And why? *So that I won't have to come to this well to draw water*, or *have to hang around the homestead and take orders from my older brother*, or *spend another day sitting in this tax office...* We can fill in the blank.

And what is God's answer to these prayers? For the Samaritan woman, it isn't a miraculous jar of water that will never run dry. For the Prodigal Son starving over a pigsty, it isn't a care package. For St. Matthew, it isn't a buyout and early retirement. For each, it is a new relationship with the One who is living bread, living water, and poorer than any

6 Josemaría Escrivá, *Friends of God* (New York: Scepter, 2002), 12.

ordinary man could ever be. Knowing him makes all the difference between hating or rebelling against our lives and finding a lamp to guide our steps in a new direction.

It is a mercy of God, albeit a painful one to receive, that he doesn't cater to what we think is the answer to our dissatisfaction with life. Our solutions are often at the surface level, meeting ego-centered needs: a craving for success and recognition, a sign that we matter in this world, results, and so forth. God refuses to feed our illusions with things that vanish like smoke (see Ps 102:3). Not that he doesn't encourage us periodically with success, but he won't indulge us with an unbroken chain of satisfactions. Sooner or later, every chain runs out of links. The Lord does not want death, our death, to be the only occasion of loss for us, so he allows lesser "deaths," even daily, to loosen our grip on the things of this world that we might lift up our hearts higher than the horizon.

"Out of the depths I cry to you, O Lord" (Ps 130:1) is how the Psalms model prayer for us, so if we feel dejected like any of these Gospel persons looking for a way out, it is time to reconnect with Jesus from those depths.

> Seek union with God and buoy yourself up with hope
> – that *sure* virtue! – because Jesus will illuminate the
> way for you with the light of his mercy, even in the
> darkest night.[7]

Seek union with God… Let that mean for you whatever

7   Escrivá, *The Forge*, 293.

it needs to mean: going to confession, making an hour of Eucharistic Adoration, being more consistent in daily prayer, going to church when you aren't "obliged" to be there. Make yourself available for the Lord's healing touch. The Shepherd who rejoices when he finds the lost lamb rejoices even more when we want to be found by him—in whatever state that might be, no matter how lost or downhearted.

St. Josemaría minces no words:

> Let's not deceive ourselves: in our life we will find vigor and victory and depression and defeat. This has always been true of the earthly pilgrimage of Christians, even of those we venerate on the altars. Don't you remember Peter, Augustine, Francis? I have never liked biographies of saints which naively — but also with a lack of sound doctrine — present their deeds as if they had been confirmed in grace from birth. No. The true life stories of Christian heroes resemble our own experience: they fought and won; they fought and lost. And then, repentant, they returned to the fray.[8]

And what did they learn upon returning to the fray? That God is faithful. That God can and does use those very side trips into failure as the material for deeper trust and hope. Otherwise, the saints would tap out and stay out. Instead, they keep coming back. "Another fall," exclaims St. Josemaría, "and what a fall! Must you give

---

8 Josemaría Escrivá, *Christ is Passing By* (New York: Scepter, 2002), 76.

up hope? No."[9] What justifies this "No"? Something far greater than willpower, something more renewable than resilience, a strength more constant than a dogged determination to succeed: it is the Light that cannot be snuffed out or suppressed, even by our repeated falls, even by our negligence and stupidity. The darkness cannot master this Light, cannot handle it, but must let it shine.

Our justification—our right—to hope comes from the Lord who does not make us wait for a sunny day before rushing to our need.

The steadfast love of the Lord never ceases,
    his mercies never come to an end;
they are new every morning;
    great is thy faithfulness.
"The Lord is my portion," says my soul,
"therefore I will hope in him." (Lamentations 3:22–24)

"Every morning" does not mean that God's mercies are available only after a twenty-four hour waiting period! No, his mercies are never-ending, always new and renewable. Or in the simple and memorable words of a contemporary religious song, "However great the sin, Mercy rushes in."[10] As soon as we've broken something, the Lord is there, ready

9 Escrivá, *The Way*, 711.

10 Carmelite Sisters of the Most Sacred Heart of Los Angeles, 2016, "Mercy Rushes In," Track 8 on *Mercy Rushes In*, Carmelite Sisters of the Most Sacred Heart of Los Angeles, compact disc.

to forgive and heal.

This biblical spirit has always been the spirit of the saints. But never think that their need for mercy was only make-believe. Never imagine that the saints are made of different stuff than we are. If we want to cultivate the same hope that buoyed them up, we must trust in the same mercy that sanctified and saved them. We need to insist on this or else risk viewing saints as quasi-superheroes, to be admired only, not imitated.

Hubert van Zeller highlights this common error, as we so easily assume that holy people don't feel the force of temptation or have no need to struggle in their spiritual journey:

> A mistake we make is to think of the saints as triumphing over temptation by the felt force of ardent love. Some of them, certainly, experienced this fire, but for most of them it has been a question of grinding out dry, hard acts of faith and hope through clenched teeth. The saints have had to fight every inch of the way against discouragement, defeatism, and even despair.[11]

Coming directly from his own experience, St. John Henry Newman affirms "Therefore I will trust Him." But listen to the circumstances in which this trust is actually forged and lived out:

> Therefore I will trust him. Whatever, wherever I am, I can never be thrown away. If I am in sickness, my sickness may serve him; in perplexity, my perplexity

---

11 Hubert van Zeller, *Approach to Calvary* (New York: Sheed and Ward, 1961), 60.

may serve him; if I am in sorrow, my sorrow may serve him. My sickness, or perplexity, or sorrow may be necessary causes of some great end, which is quite beyond us. He does nothing in vain; He may prolong my life, He may shorten it; He knows what he is about. He may take away my friends, He may throw me among strangers, he may make me feel desolate, make my spirits sink, hide the future from me—still he knows what He is about.[12]

That is not a comfortable meditation. It is the testimony of a faithful, trusting soul who knows the Lord so intimately that he can sustain all of the ways in which God acts contrary to his sense of security or stability. He knows the Lord is good, even if he himself doesn't feel particularly good about being lonely, sad, or in darkness. A deeper conviction of faith declares from the depths that "all shall be well." And that voice from the depths is not wishful thinking, but God's own Spirit interceding for us "with sighs too deep for words" (Rom 8:26).

We know that even after Christ's coming, feelings of hopelessness and abandonment, or weariness with life, can creep back into our lives—resurfacing after prolonged struggles, repeated failures, or serious disappointment. Like the sad disciples en route to Emmaus, "we had hoped" is the weary refrain of those let down on their journey. (See Luke

12 John Henry Newman, "Hope in God—Creator," in *Meditations and Devotions* (New York: Longmans, Green, & Co., 1893), 301–302.

24:13–35, especially verse 21.)

St. Josemaría's encouragement not to give up not only points to this discrepancy between our Christian ideals and our lived experience of falling short, but also to the first casualty of the conflict: hope. He offers some realistic advice. After exclaiming "How low you have fallen this time!" he calms the fallen soul: "Begin the foundations from down there. Be humble."[13] The solution to a fall is waiting for you at ground zero. Of course. If pride comes before a fall, humility always paves the way for a resurrection: *He who humbles himself will be exalted*. Don't budge from the bottom, don't even try to climb out, until you've asked the Son of God for a hand up.

Hitting bottom and finding hope waiting for us shows the gospel of Jesus Christ to be tailor-made for fallen people in a fallen world. It speaks to the tempted and the fallen, the sorrowing and despairing. Jesus described his own mission as "good news to the poor, […] release to the captives, and recovering of sight to the blind" (Lk 4:18-19), and this is the hope enkindled in us each time we look up from our own depths and make a divine rendezvous.

If this sounds fanciful or romantic, the true stories of saintly Christians confined for years in concentration camps or in prisons are proof positive that captive souls can find the Lord in ways they could not when free. From modern examples such as Ven. Francis-Xavier Nguyễn Văn Thuận, who endured

13 Escrivá, *The Way,* 712.

imprisonment for thirteen years by the communist government of Vietnam, to Walter Ciszek, SJ, who suffered more than two decades of harsh, demoralizing imprisonment in Soviet Russia, all the way back to the fourth century founder of Armenian Christianity, St. Gregory the Illuminator, left for dead in a pit for nearly fifteen years, Christ's most faithful ones learn an unquestioning trust in him by way of extreme desolation, by way of darkness.

Even the prisons that confine saints are still prisons. St. Gregory's pit remained a pit. Ven. Văn Thuận's solitary cell remained just that. Servant of God Walter Ciszek's labor camps were still a part of the Gulag system. For that matter, the stable and the manger at Bethlehem are still a cattle shed and a trough, nothing more. What makes all the difference is our receptivity to the mystery of God's will, of his inscrutable action in our lives—especially in those dark and problematic places. Without demanding to understand, we trustingly walk in the darkness of this world with only one Light to guide us: "I am the light of the world; he who follows me will not walk in darkness, but will have the light of life" (Jn 8:12).

We know how challenging it can be for us to serve such a God. We like to be in control—to kindle the fire, turn lights on or off, or slide the dimmer switch to fit our mood. Saints discover that, by enduring the dark with God, control might not be all it's cracked up to be, after all. Independence and mobility might not serve our growth as much as we give them credit for. In the end, those who sit in darkness vigilantly waiting on the Lord will behold his salvation: "He lifts up the soul and gives light to the eyes; he grants healing, life, and blessing" (Sir 34:17).

CHAPTER SIX
Counting the Stars:
Why God Allows Darkness

And he brought him outside and said, "Look toward heaven, and number the

stars, if you are able to number them."

—GENESIS 15:5

ight in the Scriptures is often a time of waiting and yearning for the Lord: "My soul waits for the Lord more than watchmen for the morning" or "I think of thee upon my bed, and meditate on thee in the watches of the night" (Ps 130:6; 63:6). The tenderness between the bride and elusive bridegroom of the Song of Solomon is likewise evocatively set within the watches of the night:

I slept, but my heart was awake.

Hark! my beloved is knocking.

"Open to me, my sister, my love,

> my dove, my perfect one;
> for my head is wet with dew,
> > my locks with the drops of the night." (Song 5:2)

But since night is firstly a privation of sunlight, we have to give the negative quality its due before searching into the positive worth of the dark hinted at here.

Night, like many "negatives" in life, is what you make of it. It can be a time of special closeness to the Lord, when "gentle silence envelope[s] all things" (Wis 18:14). But there is no denying night's peculiar power of uncaging our worst feelings and fears, making us feel powerless against the ramble of memory and imagination. "By night," says the Psalm, "[I] find no rest" (Ps 22:2). Indeed, nighttime for the sleepless can be a real torture, as the tortured Job testifies: "Nights of misery are apportioned to me. When I lie down I say, 'When shall I arise?' But the night is long, and I am full of tossing till the dawn" (Jb 7:3–4). No further explanation required.

Yes, the night is what we make of it. And yes, sometimes we are at the mercy of the night hours and can make nothing of them. But what does God make of this?

In Creation, night is willed by God as a division of time: "God separated the light from the darkness. God called the light Day, and the darkness he called Night" (Gn 1:4–5). These familiar verses might seem *too familiar* to quote, too much a part of a child's knowledge of the Bible. Romano Guardini mentions in one place how our dependence on electric or artificial light has rendered us less sensitive to the daily and seasonal alternations of light and darkness. They cease to carry much of the symbolic weight that former generations attached to them. But however familiar and simple Genesis is, a momentous truth emerges from the simplicity that often escapes us in our darker moments: God makes use of darkness. It is not a defect in creation, but a needed alternation in daily life for man to live and work in. We learn lessons of both labor and rest: "Man goes forth to his work and to his labor until the evening" (Ps 104:23), and "It is in vain that you rise up early and go late to rest, eating the bread of anxious toil; for he gives to his beloved sleep" (Ps 127:2).

But teaching mankind the proportion between work and sleep is not the main point here. In revealing himself to us in salvation history, as in our personal lives, God normally leads us from the natural to the supernatural, from things we know well to those that are lesser known (witness every parable of Jesus). If God ordinarily uses the night to give us rest, then could he not use certain kinds of spiritual darkness to *put to rest* tendencies in us that aren't helping us grow closer to him?

For one, darkness wars against our natural desire to know, to see, to understand. Some people are particularly disturbed in life by not knowing what's coming next. Planning, for them, is everything. Whatever the merits of foresight and preparation, we can only take it so far in our relationship with

God. Trying to ensure no unexpected turns can sometimes mask a lack of trust, a desire to control, and an unwillingness to walk entirely by faith. An anxious need "to make sure nothing goes wrong" can sometimes signal a deep insecurity.

Our Lady at the Annunciation comes immediately to mind. Her only question regarded the compatibility of her professed virginity with childbearing. No anxiety over what would come next, no demand for details. Yet there was darkness, even for Our Lady. But she could walk in this kind of darkness because she knew intimately him who was her light: not only the God above her, but the God growing within her.

I think again of the multiplication of the loaves. An apparently egregious lack of foresight almost resulted in an embarrassing disbanding of the thousands of gathered disciples. A failure at this moment would have emptied the ranks of the Lord's followers: Jesus had held these people in a deserted place for an imprudently long period of time and expected them to fend for themselves. So it seemed to the apostles. They were in darkness as to what God would do next and, frankly, didn't expect much. But Jesus used their understandable confusion to grow their faith and confidence. Darkness did its job because the Light of the World scattered it by the breaking of bread in his divine hands and distributing it through the apostles'.

Unplanned events in life, of course, are not the only type of darkness we know. More acute is interior darkness. That mystical literature is plentiful on this experience tells us that no one serious about the interior life may bypass it. If even Jesus could utter cries of dereliction in the garden and on the cross, we should know that he made his anguish audible for our sake. And his anguish was real.

St Anselm of Canterbury describes his soul as straining, "stand[ing] on tiptoe to see more [of God], but apart from what it has seen already, it sees nothing but darkness." Speaking directly to the Lord he admits, "Of course it does not really see darkness, because there is no darkness in you, but it sees that it can see no further because of the darkness in itself."[1] The light is simply too bright for our weak sight, as looking into the sun blinds the naked eye. But it is this light-in-darkness and darkness-in-light that occupies much of the mystical journey, as so many of the saints report.

Risking oversimplification, I will only summarize here what saints and doctors like St. John of the Cross have already explored so exhaustively. But sometimes a summary is just what we need when plunging into the volumes of the great masters is not practical or possible. Perhaps even more timely is some preview of the terrain the soul will inevitably cover, so that when we hit the arid plains we will have some compass to walk by.

---

1   Anselm of Canterbury, *Proslogion*, in *Opera omnia*, edit. Schmitt, Seccovii, 1938, chap. 14, 16, 26; 1, 111–113, 121–122, in *Liturgy of the Hours*, vol. 2, pp. 1774–1776.

Since God is infinitely above us, and yet closer to us than we are to ourselves, we cannot cling to ideas and images of him that limit who he is. It is another way of saying that we cannot see divine things clearly unless we come to recognize that, unaided by grace, we cannot see them at all. Even better is St. Augustine's pithy comment: "If you understand him, he is not God."[2]

To comprehend something is, in a way, to master it, to put it into a category of knowledge. And although we can say much about God based on what he reveals about himself through Scripture and nature, what we know is always less than what we don't know. His mystery is certainly no less mysterious than even we, finite beings, are to ourselves or our neighbor to us. The Book of Judith asks this pointed question:

> You cannot plumb the depths of the human heart, nor find out what a man is thinking; how do you expect to search out God, who made all these things, and find out his mind or comprehend his thought? (Jdt 8:14)

If our God is truly a God who hides himself (see Is 45:15), it is because divine hiddenness better reveals who God is than spectacular and even violent showings of his power. Consider Elijah and Moses: Elijah stood and witnessed terrifying phenomena from his cave in Mount Horeb (see 1 Kgs 19:9–13). Each one of the marvels would have been enough to demonstrate the presence and power of God, yet

2   Augustine of Hippo, Sermon 52, 16; PL 38, 360

it was only a whispering voice that finally drew Elijah to the mouth of the cave to converse with the Lord. He recognized it—not the wind, earthquake, or fire—as the authentic voice of God. Or centuries earlier when God revealed himself to Moses, the phenomenon was very simple and humble: a burning bush unconsumed by the flames enveloping its leaves and branches. It was enough to get Moses' attention, enough to make him fear the Lord: "And Moses hid his face, for he was afraid to look at God" (Ex 3:6).

To us, it might seem better with miracles and signs abounding. After all, aren't they performed to inspire belief? Surely they are. But whatever faith they inspire in the moment is not enough to sustain one's faith for a lifetime. Jesus considers "evil and adulterous" the generation that demands signs of him (see Mt 12:39). Sought for the wrong reason, signs can in fact be testimony against you, as the Exodus generation learned.

Witnessing—even marveling—over signs from heaven, as many did during the Lord's public ministry, did not prevent some of those same people from plotting or at least acquiescing to his death. Nor do those escape his condemnation who claim, "Lord, Lord, did we not prophesy in your name, and cast out demons in your name, and do many mighty works in your name?" Jesus warns them, "Not everyone who says to me, 'Lord, Lord,' shall enter the kingdom of heaven, but he who does the will of my Father who is in heaven" (Mt 7:21–23).

Faith needs to develop from mere association with Jesus, a tagging along at the edge of the crowd ("I was there when he did that"), to the personal, prayerful relationship of intimate knowledge. And such knowledge can only be acquired in secret, in the dark, where my heart is naked and exposed before God, where my desires are tested and I am found to be what I truly am: deep or shallow, self-centered or surrendered. In the dark, all of our unworthy motivations appear before us like unsubstantial ghosts, which we had thought solid enough in the daylight. And perhaps they frighten us as ghosts do, revealing our hidden vanities, pride, and self-seeking. But if we let him, God will reduce the soul to simplicity, honesty, and utter humility by his purifying darkness. In our trusting submission, we learn to know the Lord as the One who tenderly cares for our soul—yet how surprising that the intimate knowledge should come through something as violent as the painful stripping of our soul! But so deft are the hands of the Divine Physician that he heals as he wounds: "For he wounds, but he binds up; he smites, but his hands heal" (Jb 5:18).

What this interior darkness amounts to is a replaying of all that the Israelites experienced in their desert sojourn to the Promised Land:

And you shall remember all the way which the Lord your God has led you these forty years in the wilderness, that he might humble you, testing you to know what was in your heart, whether you would keep his commandments, or not. (Dt 8:2)

The Test of Interior Darkness

Normally we think our word is good enough. If God wants to know whether our hearts are pure, whether we are obedient, whether we will follow him in faith, all he needs to do is ask, right? Our lack of self-knowledge pipes up before we've thought better: *I really don't know what's in my heart. I really don't know what I'm capable of unless the Lord tests me.* On the day Israel marched out of Egypt, not one of them dreamed that Caleb and Joshua would be the only ones of that generation to cross the border into the Promised Land. All had been at the heart of the most extraordinary signs that God had ever wrought, as he upended the religious and political culture of Egypt, most especially in bringing about the first Passover. No one would have believed that the very people for whom those miracles had been done would die in the wilderness as a punishment for not trusting that God could bring them into the land flowing with milk and honey (see Nm 14:26–35). Yet that is what happened.

> None of the men who have seen my glory and my signs which I wrought in Egypt and in the wilderness, and yet have put me to the proof these ten times and have not hearkened to my voice, shall see the land which I swore to give to their fathers; and none of those who despised me shall see it. (Nm 14:22–23)

In the concrete, this test of interior darkness shows itself as either a personal distaste for or a lack of comfort in spiritual things, prayer, even the sacraments. Think again of the Israelites: their boredom and even disgust for the food which God had provided for them was directed at the very manna which had rained down from heaven to sustain them ("O that we had meat to eat! [...] [But] there is nothing at all but this manna to look at" [Nm 11:4, 6]). It was not only good, but the "food of angels," for which the people did not have to work, but which was "ready to eat, providing every pleasure and suited to every taste" (Wis 16:20). But it had grown too familiar to their taste.

For our part, we know spiritual practices to be good and holy. We do not cease to avail ourselves of them. But the motives of consolation and joy that had previously kept us riveted to a pew or lost in hours of Adoration seem to have dried up, seem to be gone for good. Provided we are not at fault through unrepentant sin or laziness, this is God's darkness surrounding the soul. And what does he expect us to do with it? How can we pray if it not only feels dry and distracted, but also like a positive waste of time?

It is not enough to promise future consolations if we just hang in there. What God is doing is strengthening the soul to love, believe, and hope—independent of feelings. As we observed earlier, it is easy to operate on the assumption that feelings tell the whole story about reality: the more intense our feelings, the truer our perceptions must be. So that if we begin to feel bad about ourselves, about our spirituality, then our spiritual practices must be vain, our efforts worthless. We must have been deluded, or God must be far away. That is, at least, how the whole thing makes us feel.

But couldn't the Lord be teaching us to know him now in a deeper way? Couldn't the pain and confusion be the necessary ingredients for a more authentic faith, hope, and love? As God reduces us in order to manifest the contents of our hearts, we are confronted with humbling truths that compel choices: should we stick around and let God trim away our dead outgrowths, or should we scrap the whole project and, I don't know, go out for ice cream?

What feels like the demolition of self is, in reality, the upbuilding of our true self. What seems to diminish us to the point of practical despair is actually the Lord shoring up a surer foundation for our selfhood. The importance of this cannot be overestimated. If the Pharisee and tax collector each came before God with a story to tell about themselves, only one of them told (or knew) the true story— even if it was brief and repetitive: "God, be merciful to me a sinner!" (Lk18:13). If in the end our whole life is really the story of God's mercies, then there's nothing more to add. The tax collector had allowed God to bring him through the darkness of his moral character, and that journey had borne two extremely important fruits in the spiritual life:

humility and trust.

When we have been brought down through the many layers of self, having maintained a firm grip on the Lord all the while, we attain true peace, freedom in humility, and implicit trust ever after in God's guidance. We reach the dawn.

We are like Dante emerging from the darkest circles of the underworld, accompanied not by the laurel-crowned Virgil, but by the royal Son of God.

> My guide and I entered that hidden road
> to make our way back up to the bright world.
> We never thought of resting while we climbed.
> We climbed, he first and I behind, until,
> through a small round opening ahead of us
> I saw the lovely things the heavens hold,
> and we came out to see once more the stars.[3]

Once more the stars shine, appearing more beautiful to our eyes than before. Have they always been so numerous and glorious? The stars have not changed, but we have. Our inner vision purified and transformed, we see not so much *more* as *truly*. More clearly than ever, we see the deceptiveness of self-reliance, of trusting overmuch in feelings and perceptions. The avenues of knowledge we normally depend upon (such as the senses) have only a limited value in the spiritual life.

---

3 Dante Alighieri, *The Divine Comedy,* Vol. 1: *Inferno*, Canto XXXIV, trans. Mark Musa (New York: Penguin Books, 2003), 383.

What is needed is love, love relearned and reexperienced through intimate union with God. Through leaning on him and patiently allowing him to purify our hearts, we learn the otherwise unknowable truth of life in death, of security in weakness:

> For his sake I have suffered the loss of all things, and count them as refuse, […] that I may know him and the power of his resurrection, and may share his sufferings, becoming like him in his death, that if possible I may attain the resurrection from the dead. (Phil 3:8, 10–11)

If the Crucifixion and the experience of the small band of disciples on Calvary teaches us anything, it is this love at the heart of darkness and dereliction. Even if, as St. John of the Cross says, we feel like we're getting lost in the darkness, we can walk on no surer path than behind our Savior, though it goes through a death-dark valley to an unknown country.

> To reach a new and unknown land and journey along unknown roads, travelers cannot be guided by their own knowledge; instead, they have doubts about their own knowledge and seek the guidance of others. Obviously they cannot reach new territory or attain this added knowledge if they do not take these new and unknown roads and abandon those familiar ones. Similarly, people learning new details about their art or trade must work in darkness and not with what they already know. If they refuse to lay aside their former knowledge, they will never make any further progress.

The soul, too, when it advances, walks in darkness and unknowing.[4]

In our walk of faith, we move beyond signs and images toward the real Object of our faith, hope, and love. The divine darkness alone can prepare us for this encounter, when nothing of self is left, no obstacle remains, and the light of our eyes is all him.

4   John of the Cross, *The Dark Night*, Book 2, 16.8, in *The Collected Works of St. John of the Cross*, trans. Kieran Kavanaugh, OCD, and Otilio Rodriguez, OCD (Washington, DC.: ICS, 1991), 433.

CHAPTER SEVEN
The Night Will Be My Light

...and night shall be my light in my pleasures.

—PSALM 138:11[1]

aving sketched the dark itinerary traversed by souls in their journey toward God, our thumbnail odyssey brought us to pause at the predawn stars. The heavenly lights appear clearer, more beautiful and refreshing, after a nocturnal sojourn through obscurity and desolation. A condensed, but proportionally intense, summary of the night of faith could well be taken from Abraham's supreme test of faith and obedience (see Gen 22:1–19). Romano Guardini thus describes it:

> When the darkness of the ordeal surrounded [Abraham]
> he must have felt he was engulfed in blind darkness,

---

1   Douay-Rheims 1899 American Edition. The numbering of the psalms in this translation differs from what is commonly used today. Psalm 138 here corresponds to Psalm 139 in more contemporary translations.

alone in his hopeless affliction. But now the dark walls fell and he realized that he had not been forsaken but had been standing in the sight of God.[2]

It's impossible to overstress this. If even darkness is not dark for God, then even in our blackest moments, our faith should assure us that we are seen. *Seen*, but not as by a spectator. To be seen by God means more than that he's generally aware that we exist, that he's following the stats of our life from afar the way people follow other people, sports, stocks, and politics on the internet. It means even more than having a sympathetic audience cheering us on or grieving when we fail. His sight, or knowledge, means complete penetration of our being by love. Monsignor Guardini characterizes it as "an act of love. With His seeing He embraces His creatures, affirms them, and encourages them, since He hates nothing that He has created."[3]

Abraham may have felt "surrounded" or "engulfed" by darkness, but God was deeper in Abraham than Abraham's own thoughts about what God was asking of him. The Lord was inside him, moving Abraham to say yes, to act, to go through with it, even though it was the sacrifice of the one thing that gave his life meaning, the one promise that had kept him hoping and obeying: the birth of an heir, Isaac, the promised son.

2   Guardini, *The Living God*, 29.

3   Guardini, *The Living God*, 34.

Abraham's whole impetus for leaving both homeland and kin was this promised heir, through whom a multitudinous progeny would spring (the number of which God compared to those same stars we have just contemplated). And now God is telling him to kill the very fulfillment of his promise?

Yes. That is the thickest darkness imaginable. To have sojourned through strange places and dangers, establishing oneself in a foreign land beset with warring tribes—and to have waited and waited and waited. And what does it all amount to? A hoax? A delusion? A divine runaround? No. Listen to the faith that undergirded the promptness of Abraham's obedience:

> By faith Abraham, when he was tested, offered up Isaac, and he who had received the promises was ready to offer up his only son, of whom it was said, "Through Isaac shall your descendants be named." He considered that God was able to raise men even from the dead; hence he did receive him back, and this was a symbol. (Heb 11:17–19)

Yes. And this is the greatest faith imaginable. Faith is nothing if not bold, and Abraham rises to the occasion. He is used to bartering and arguing with the Lord, holding back neither frustration nor complaint, and submitting in blind faith to God's leading promises, even as childless years rolled by. But Abraham holds God to his promises, so that even if God commands the slaying of the very one his life centers around, Abraham is certain that Isaac will be brought back. Since God had earmarked Isaac as the one and only heir, there would be no further negotiations. Death would have to lead to resurrection.

Surrendering what you most cherish is a specifically divine test. Only God can make this kind of demand of us because any lesser thing we cling to, no matter how good it is, we must detach from—in spirit, at least, if not in fact. Jesus calls disciples to abandon their livelihoods, property, prospects for marriage, and follow him. And he gets away with it. He tells us that we may love nothing—not our own life, nor parents, nor children—more than him. And he realistically expects obedience from people such as us, even with all of our weaknesses, failures, and divided affections. Only One who is supreme goodness and love can make such demands and expect not only a cautious response, but a generous one.

The many good things the Lord has created for our use and enjoyment can become obstacles to our love for God if they are loved for their own sake. If we serve God for anything less than himself, our spiritual life will suffer periodic collapse, a breakdown of greater or lesser extent, which God, in his infinite mercy, allows in order to return us to himself in a more authentic way. And if we are left feeling empty and confused, and maybe embarrassed by our self-deception, when a motive we've been operating with eventually runs its course, we must not lose heart. God is used to working with imperfect motives—with imperfect everything. Even Abraham faltered several times, as did Moses, David, the apostles...

The spiritual night, then, the night of tests and perplexity, cannot be advertised as "romantic." It means a painful privation of sight, not the measured dimming of light that creates an ideal ambience. I nevertheless claimed a positive value to the night in the last chapter, evidenced by passages from the Psalms, the Song of Solomon, and (we may add) several of the Lord's parables of vigilant servants and handmaids. The positive character of spiritual night is not, again, a matter of enjoying an ideal setting lit by starlight or candlelight. Darkness is more than just a filler between glittering things. But neither is it an end in itself, and it is under the aspect of its spiritual utility that darkness' worth is best considered.

Peeking ahead at the answers in the back of the book to see where the night is taking us, the simple words of a saint who wrote from the other side of this night say it all: "Union with God through love"[4] is the end to which St. John of the Cross points before showing us, more exhaustively than anyone, the map that leads to it. We have already depended on St. John of the Cross to guide us "along the unknown roads" of the spirit and will continue to lean on him in this chapter as well. Authority in spiritual matters is key, as most of us don't

4   John of the Cross, *The Dark Night*, Book 1, 8.1, 375.

know what we're talking about or how to guide others unless we ourselves have been directed by someone, like St. John of the Cross, who knows the way not from theory alone, but from having walked it.

The holy Carmelite designates two "nights" through which we must pass in order to reach perfect union with God through love: one of the senses and one of the spirit. The night of the senses purifies our bodily senses, but is not aimed simply at curbing our indulgent passions and appetites. St. John of the Cross says that the prerequisite for entering the night of sense is a prior resolution to mortify our appetite for worldly things (which encompasses the threefold concupiscence of "the lust of the flesh and the lust of the eyes and the pride of life" [1 Jn 2:16]). Once that is underway, a purification of our appetite for spiritual joy and consolation begins. Although God ordinarily attracts us to pursue prayer and the spiritual life by delight in spiritual things, he will not allow us to rest in that comfort forever. These are only holy enticements intended to wean us away from delight in worldly amusements so that we might acquire a taste for the sweetness of the Lord.

We all know how eagerly we will keep doing something as long as it is pleasant and rewarding. Once it becomes arduous, the real test of our motivations begins. And since God cannot be served only outwardly—indeed, he severely censures those whose mouths are full of piety but whose hearts are distant from him—he begins the purification of our relationship with him by withdrawing the good feelings that once attended our prayer, our participation in the sacred liturgy, retreats, and so on. It is the perennial experience of honeymoon's end and the beginning of real, day-to-day married life.

Having persevered through this kind of desolation, a deeper purification of the spirit follows: the night of the spirit. St. John of the Cross very logically teaches that since the bad habits residing in our senses are rooted in the soul, a radical uprooting must take place there as well, in the deepest part of our being. This is where darkness becomes most acute:

> Wishing to strip them [...] of this old self and clothe them with the new, which is created according to God in the newness of sense, as the Apostle says [Col 3:9–10; Eph 4:22–24; Rom 12:2], God divests the faculties, affections, and senses, both spiritual and sensory, interior and exterior. He leaves the intellect in darkness, the will in aridity, the memory in emptiness, and the affections in supreme affliction, bitterness, and anguish by depriving the soul of the feeling and satisfaction it previously obtained from spiritual blessings. For this privation is one of the conditions required that the spiritual form, which is the union of love, may be introduced into the spirit and united with it.[5]

All of this, remember, is for the sake of *union with God through love*. But if it seems too complicated and negative, we

5   John of the Cross, *The Dark Night*, Book 2, 3.3, 399.

have the gospel to remind us of the general call to salvation, which passes by a constricted road:

> Enter by the narrow gate; for the gate is wide and the way is easy, that leads to destruction, and those who enter by it are many. For the gate is narrow and the way is hard, that leads to life, and those who find it are few. (Mt 7:13–14)

What our Lord says of eternal life is no less true about the spiritual means we employ to get there. A part of the narrowness and difficulty of the road is precisely the exacting work of purification of which St. John of the Cross speaks (which is nothing other than gospel teaching re-presented in mystical terms). But lest anyone get the wrong impression, we are not saying that God sets before us two indistinguishable paths, and we had better hope we find the right one; nor are we saying that God abandons us to fend for ourselves once we've set our feet on the narrow way. The apparent complexity and certain difficulty of the way is God's way of bringing a cry for help from our hearts.

St. Peter was firmly planted on the narrow path when he began walking on water toward Jesus. He was walking by faith, an imperfect faith, but with a genuine confidence in Jesus. His cry "Lord, save me!" as he sank is the cry of one recognizing his complete human inability to do a divine work. Our salvation, our spiritual life, our sanctification, are preeminently divine works. And Jesus is not just planning to meet us on the other side of the narrow gate or dark night, if we happen to make it. He wants to accompany us from starting gate to finish line, to be what he came to be for us: Jesus, our Savior.

To refuse this path is to imperil our salvation, not to mention stunting the rich spiritual growth we are all capable of. It also suggests a very inadequate understanding of our human and Christian vocation: we were born for union with God through love. That is our happiness, in time and in eternity. Like the stone that falls earthward, we are set on a Godward course along which we can allow ourselves to be drawn or from which we can fall away. A stone falls inevitably down, but we do not go inevitably to the Lord. Although Christ draws all things to himself, not all follow the pull. It is the roughness of the road and the utter darkness of the night, says St. John of the Cross, that makes most people either slow down or stop all together.

Yet once we realize the necessary work the night is doing, how it is preparing our souls for a love and union deeper than we have ever known, we just might keep at it, knowing that we are fulfilling our very reason for existing. Why any night of sense or spirit is necessary is owing to the disorders in the soul, put there by original sin and exacerbated by actual sin. We need to be bent back into shape, so to speak. Our desires need divesting of self-interest, and only persevering on the hard road of renunciation can accomplish that.

Meeting God in this dark night is perhaps nowhere better described than in St. John of the Cross' famous poem of the same name, "The Dark Night." His sheer passion for darkness and night is infectious, making one want to deny oneself anything to reach this place of total freedom, total abandonment in God. He describes his soul as a stilled house, having reached the quiet of the night, and free to seek the Beloved with no light other than faith.

How does this mean freedom for the soul? Having denied itself, denuded itself, of every hindrance to its relationship with the Lord, it is unencumbered by any attachment. The soul is free to follow him, free to love, free to give—no strings attached.

One stanza stands out in particular:

O guiding night!
O night more lovely than the dawn!
O night that has united
the Lover with his beloved,
transforming the beloved in her Lover.[6]

Night is paradoxically the guide to God; night is the womb in which the soul is transformed into a new creation in God; the night unites the freed soul with the transcendently free Lord of Hosts. Only in such complete freedom can the truest and best love be shared. No shadow of self-interest, no will

6 John of the Cross, "The Dark Night," in *The Dark Night*, stanza 5, 359.

to dominate, no vying to prove oneself. The night has done its sweet and painstaking work.

Enchanting and excruciating, the night is a divine remedy, a surgery in the soul. And it is undergone not for any crass desire for a payoff in the end, but with the assurance that God is remaking the soul to its original beauty and innocence. He is rendering us capable of deep union with him. The beginning devotion of the spiritual life is very good, and in a sense should never be completely abandoned. But the Lord loves us too much to leave us at a superficial level of spirituality. Sooner or later, he challenges, withdraws, keeps silent, seems to leave us all to ourselves. Then the battle of love begins. At one and the same time it is courtship, standoff, pursuing, hiding, hinting, attracting, unknowing, and understanding. It is Abraham all over again.

In the 2011 motion picture on the life of St. Josemaría Escrivá, *There Be Dragons*, a fictional dialogue transpires between St. Josemaría and a mysterious young woman (Aline) in the insane asylum where the saint is hiding out. She surprises him in prayer and reveals her own way of grappling with God in silence and darkness.

> *Aline*: He doesn't hear you, does he? All this pain, and God just stays silent. He is a monster, you know?
> I love him.
> *Josemaría*: Although he's a monster?
> *Aline*: Women can love monsters. […]

After I was raped, I stopped going to Mass. I couldn't understand how God allowed such a thing. I accepted, you see, God can be terrible. So now I do go to Mass, and my prayers are deeper than before. I fight him with love, you see. Like you.

You look me in the eye. You don't pity me.

Josemaría: No. No, you are extremely brave.

Aline: Not really. I still sleep with the lights on... and a chair wedged under the door handle.

I think you have mountains to climb. And I think it will be painful. But that will make it seem sweet when you are finished.[7]

Aline's initially disturbing account leads Josemaría to understand God's will as encompassing real tragedy, real trauma, as he contemplates God's will for himself in the midst of civil war. And yet, the even broader providence in which evil is used for good stands tall: enduring the darkness, ascending the mountain, and surrendering to the Lord's inscrutable designs culminates in a sweet consummation. Love is reborn, stronger than before, because it has passed by way of the cross.

The *union with God through love* of St. John of the Cross is not bought cheaply. Although we cannot know the ultimate purposes of all the evils we sustain here below, we can be certain that if we allow them to drive us further into the arms

7   *There Be Dragons*, written and directed by Roland Joffé (Madrid: Morena Films, 2011), DVD.

of God, deeper into trust, then they will not have defeated us. It is characteristic of the saints that although they suffer mightily they do not allow evil to destroy their faith, hope, and love.

St. John of the Cross was unjustly imprisoned by his own friars for eight months in a cell measuring ten by six feet. He was beaten, given barely any food, and suffered many other indignities. It was there that he wrote some of his magnificent poetry, including much of "The Spiritual Canticle." Listen to the strains of love issuing from a dark, cramped cell:

Extinguish these miseries,

since no one else can stamp them out;

and may my eyes behold you,

because you are their light,

and I would open them to you alone.

Reveal your presence,

and may the vision of your beauty be my death;

for the sickness of love

is not cured

except by your very presence and image.[8]

We must listen, too, to the sounds coming from our own hearts as God cleanses our souls so that our souls' love may be as free and expansive as this. Are we struggling with God,

8   John of the Cross, "The Spiritual Canticle," in *The Collected Works of St. John of the Cross*, trans. Kieran Kavanaugh, OCD, and Otilio Rodriguez, OCD (Washington, DC: ICS, 1991), stanzas 10–11, 472–473.

resisting, sorrowing at what he takes from us? Where he is leaving us? To be sure, it is painful. But we must be even more assured: the pain endured in reaching union with God will make it seem sweet when we are finished.

CHAPTER EIGHT
The Glory to Be Revealed

I consider that the sufferings of this present time are not worth comparing with the glory that is to be revealed to us.

—ROMANS 8:18

I f the spiritual night is a prelude to deepening union with God, could not the darkness of a blind man presage a numinous vision—a vision whose only adequate preparation is the total absence of light from birth? Darkness as a prologue to the sight of God is the special prerogative of the man known only as the "man blind from his birth" in the Gospel of John (see Jn 9). In barely the space of an hour, he goes from a blind beggar to an adorer, kneeling in worship before the Son of God.

Glory was revealed to him—not the ultimate glory of heaven, but "the glory of God in the face of Christ" (2 Cor 4:6). He saw Jesus' face and was prepared to worship him as

God. *Prepared* is the operative word. He is not simply humbled before the miraculous power of Jesus, as amazing as the healing was, but his affliction had disposed him to see God in an extraordinary way. The man was evidently accepting of his condition, and so had learned to depend on others and to work within his limitations. He is so clearly docile when Jesus anoints his eyes with clay and sends him to wash in the pool of Siloam—a pool situated outside the city walls, perhaps involving a walk of some distance for the man. But he did it without protest.

All of this shows a purpose behind suffering that only the gospel can fully open to us.

Before the dramatic and earthy healing of the blind man creates an uproar in the vicinity of the temple, before God kneels down to scoop a bit of dirt to make an unusual clay ointment with his saliva, the apostles ask Jesus an offhand question that reveals an assumption that many probably share: physical suffering is inevitably linked to personal sin.

"Rabbi, who sinned, this man or his parents, that he was born blind?" (Jn 9:2). They don't ask *if* blindness is the result of sin; they ask *who* sinned. Sometimes, no doubt, it is true that we suffer in body or mind because we've done wrong at some point. Our Lord's warning to the paralytic at the pool of Bethesda confirms this: "See, you are well! Sin no more, that nothing worse befall you" (Jn 5:14). Illness may indeed be a way of atoning for sin, or at least of cooling our heels to prevent future wrongdoing. God does whatever he needs to do to keep us from drifting too far.

But we've left out another extremely important and mysterious possibility that only the Lord Jesus could teach us: the glory of God. "It was not that this man sinned, or his parents," Jesus tells the apostles, "but that the works of God might be made manifest in him" (Jn 9:3). Glory combines notoriety and acclaim, fame and praise. Thus when God's works are made manifest, they are magnified or celebrated by those of goodwill. Those of ill will (e.g., Exodus' Pharaoh and the New Testament's Pharisees) only harden their hearts and seek to erase the good done, as when the Lord's enemies sought to kill Lazarus whom the Lord had raised.

Suffering and humiliation, especially in St. John's Gospel, are tightly knit to glory, as when Jesus associates his death with glorification:

> The hour has come for the Son of man to be glorified. Truly, truly, I say to you, unless a grain of wheat falls into the earth and dies, it remains alone; but if it dies, it bears much fruit. (Jn 12:23–24)

The Lord knows exactly who this blind man is, who his parents are, the whole backstory. And so he tells us, in effect: *I orchestrated this so as to manifest the glory of God.* And in the end, that is exactly what happens. Not only is the man healed, but he comes to explicit faith in Christ: "[Jesus asked,] 'Do you believe in the Son of man?' [...] He said, 'Lord, I believe';

and he worshiped him" (Jn 9:35, 38). In brief, that is the whole story. But it is unlike other miraculous healings in that Jesus gives the reason for the debility, and it is not the reason anyone expected.

As Christians, we have come to rely upon and expect the help (even the miraculous help) of Our Lady and the saints. They always hear our prayers and often honor our requests with the "expected" results. And so we give glory to God for the intercession of his holy ones on our behalf. But apart from miraculous healings, apart from any healing at all, is not the story of the man blind from birth our story as well?

Imagine the conversation between Jesus and the apostles is about us. Imagine they make this observation about us: *Lord, did they sin or did their parents sin, that they ended up this way?* And instead of blindness, insert our biggest problem, our thickest darkness. Maybe our biggest problem *is* the result of sin. But even if it is, it doesn't change the Lord's answer: "But that the works of God might be made manifest in him." It is often observed by the saints that God's greatest work is, in fact, the conversion of a sinner into a saint, causing all of heaven to rejoice.

Thus, God permits physical and even moral evils in our lives in order to manifest his glory, his works. This is an inscrutable truth demanding deep reflection. We may not always draw a straight line between suffering and God's glory in our lives, but faith convinces us of the link—and we need not be so adept at assembling the puzzle pieces. Calculating and connecting were the furthest thing from the mind of the man born blind (he is easily one of the most *uncalculating* persons in the Gospels): "Whether [Jesus] is a sinner, I do not know;" he replies to those seeking to condemn Jesus, "one thing I know, that though I was blind, now I see" (Jn 9:25).

God has made us with an extraordinary capacity for giving him a unique glory that no one else can give. We exist, says St. Paul, "for the praise of his glory" (Eph 1:12).

We should not imagine that the vocation to praise God's glory is the same as hymn singing on Sunday. It comes from the experience of salvation, of rescue when we had thought we were as good as lost. In other words, in our firsthand experience of personal weakness, failure, and debility, we recognize that self-salvation is a doomed enterprise. And as we are begging for alms, having become poor in spirit, we are ready to receive the saving grace upon which our praise will sound forth: "… to the praise of his glorious grace which he freely bestowed on us in the Beloved" (Eph 1:6).

It is easy to see ourselves as victims of circumstance, of *bad luck*, instead of vessels of glory. That's not too surprising. How many of us go around habitually feeling *glorious*? Most of the time, we are probably more aware of how fragile we are and how prone to fail, miscalculate, or get it wrong in some way. So when things do go wrong, it is more or less what we expected.

But glory, in any case, is not a feeling. It is the radiance a soul gives off after God has touched it, changed it, healed it. Sometimes the radiance is a song of praise or a testimonial of mercy. Most of the time, though, it shows itself in a person's quiet but joyful selflessness, in imitation of the Divine Master. We could apply words that St. Peter addresses to Christian women to all who give glory to God: "Let not yours be the outward adorning [...] but let it be the hidden person of the heart with the imperishable jewel of a gentle and quiet spirit, which in God's sight is very precious" (1 Pt 3:3–4).

Taking our cue from the gospel, then, we ask questions that revolutionize the character of whatever we're going through. Instead of "Why us?" it becomes: "What are the works of God that God is manifesting? What generosity, what courage, what patience, is the Lord drawing out of this *unideal* self in this *unideal* place at this *unideal* time?" It might not be anything exciting. It probably will not be like the heroic, unrepeatable moment when St. Maximilian Kolbe stepped forward and took the place of a Jewish prisoner randomly chosen to die in Auschwitz. Although that was an exceptional response to an extraordinary grace, St. Maximilian had been preparing in lesser ways for such a moment his whole life.

It is normally in those lesser (but not unimportant) things that we have to seek the answers to our questions. The Lord is likely only calling an ordinary virtue out of us. But virtues are the stuff of our moral life, upon which our spiritual life rises or falls. St. Teresa of Avila insists on the need for practicing virtue (humility most especially) if one desires to advance in the ways of prayer, although she does not demand of others (much less of herself!) perfection in virtue before we can get anywhere in the spiritual life.

Regarding contemplative prayer, she declares: "I say that the King of glory will not come to our soul—I mean to be united with it—if we do not make the effort to gain the great virtues."[1] So we cannot minimize what appears minor at first glance. Lesser virtues pave the way for the greater, and God is not stingy in rewarding us with deeper and deeper draughts of his Spirit the more we strive to grow in the likeness of Christ and his saints.

The general point here is to look at our lives, especially the dark and awkward parts, imbued with a sense of Divine Providence. Whatever the circumstance that draws a response out of us, be it suffering or anger or fear or annoyance, the bedrock issue is God's providence, God's intentions for us. If we never ask the question of what he wants, will we ever find our way out of the darkness?

Amusement parks or traveling circuses, formerly common in the states, sometimes feature a hall of mirrors among the attractions. Just when we think we're making headway along a

1 Teresa of Avila, *The Way of Perfection*, in *The Collected Works of St. Teresa of Avila*, vol. 2, trans. Kieran Kavanaugh, OCD, and Otilio Rodriguez, OCD (Washington, DC: ICS, 1987), 16.6, 95.

passage, we meet ourselves—our own excited or exasperated reflection staring right back at us. I wonder if this is how life can become if we remain enclosed in a world where God's purposes for us are rarely if ever considered. We keep meeting ourselves, each time a little more puzzled or anxious as we try to find our way free.

The Demands of Sight

Our willingness to consider, even to surrender to, life as issuing each moment from God's hands is how he causes light to shine out of darkness again and again. Creation is not the only moment when God floods utter blackness with radiance. Much like the Lord's own tomb (where one expects only corruption, perfect life comes forth), our own place of darkness can give birth to good qualities we never thought we possessed. Someone with no inclination to leadership and organization is suddenly called upon to lead and rises to the occasion. Another who shies away from conflict steps forward to resolve a dispute or to defend the weak. Or a person afraid of suffering finally learns how to suffer with confidence in God. The difficulty, the darkness, is the setting out of which new light comes.

Thus, if Jesus in a real sense "orchestrated" this miracle by permitting this man to be blind from birth, then he certainly put him (and his parents) on an extremely difficult path. Many adjustments had to be made for him as a child, greater responsibility and vigilance for everyone involved in his care. The little one had to learn how to walk in the dark, to feel his way, listen to cues, and avail himself of the kindness of others. Was he ever mistreated by other boys? Were jokes played on him to make him confused or even to trip and fall? We can't exclude any of this.

But when we meet him as an adult beggar we notice something right away: he is not embittered by his plight. He neither curses God nor blames anyone. He is utterly docile and simple, strikingly so. The lessons the Lord has been teaching him his whole life long bear the desired fruit: trust in God and confidence in his providence. This is no Barabbas, characterized by the Gospels as a murderer and robber, giving no indication that, once freed, he would amend his life. The man born blind, freed from blindness, is prepared to respond to the mercy he has received—not so much in repentance as in an embracing of all of the beautiful demands a life of sight now presents to him.

A detail of this miracle which is always very striking— striking because it is so ordinary—is the application of mud to the blind man's eyes. Our Lord chooses to heal by means of mud. We should meditate on that. Ordinary mud, the stuff we scrape off of our shoes, the stuff we try to step over. Jesus took common dirt, mixed it with his own saliva, and smeared it upon the blind man's eyes.

To me it sounds a bit like St. Bernadette on her hands and

knees in Lourdes, digging through the mud in search of a miraculous clear stream of water. Everyone stands around pitying her, telling her parents to drag her back home for the spectacle she's creating. Yet she is undeterred in what looks like madness. But trusting the "Lady in white," she finds a clear-flowing and healing miracle in the mud.

I wonder if sometimes our souls stay sick or blind simply because we aren't receiving the healing that God keeps providing in the very things that provoke our annoyance.

Jesus heals us in ways we don't expect, ask for, or understand—in ways that seem too simple or even inefficient. There is nothing curative about saliva, dirt, mud, and a pool of water. But when the Son of God makes use of them, they become instruments of restoration. Rather than simply issuing the command, "Receive your sight," Jesus troubles himself to make a remedy, to show us that by very ordinary means he will heal us.

And by "healing" we mean something other than the restoration of a faculty, something perhaps less noticeable but more in keeping with the Lord's saving mission. It may find its best illustration in another story of healing, that of the paralytic who was cleverly let down by his friends through the roof of the place where Jesus was teaching (Lk 5:17–26). The commotion in the packed room must have been great with the sudden opening of the roof and slow descent of a man bound to a stretcher. Cheers and laughter probably mixed with some disapproval. But all were waiting to see what Jesus would do. "Man, your sins are forgiven you," was the Lord's response (Lk 5:20). Not what anyone was expecting.

In saying this, he demonstrates the priority of the soul over the body. The reconciliation of souls to God was the reason Jesus came to die. This is not to downgrade the human body at all, but to underscore how it shares the destiny of the soul, rising again at the end of time, whether one is saved or lost. But its destiny hinges entirely on the soul's state upon death.

Only after Jesus catches everyone off guard with the forgiveness of sins does he heal the paralytic. He proves that even in virtue of his humanity, he has the authority to do what is normally reserved to God alone: the forgiveness of sins. It is easier to say something unprovable (like "your sins are forgiven") than to do what cannot be disproved: restoring mobility to the limbs of one completely bereft of their use. And the people fittingly reply, *glorifying God*: "And amazement seized them all, and they glorified God and were filled with awe, saying, 'We have seen strange things today.'" (Lk5:26) *They glorified God*.

When the impossible happens to our blind friend from the temple, the people (including his parents) don't know what to do. All seem too petrified to do what comes naturally: praise the Lord. His parents, and most others, were reluctant to acknowledge Christ publicly for fear of being excommunicated from the synagogue (see Jn 9:22). Indeed, the Lord's enemies were prepared to condemn him, the healed man, and everything about the healing: it wasn't the right time, right place, or right person. They would prefer that he remain a blind beggar. Perhaps most tellingly of all, the Evangelist underscores the timing of the healing: it was a Sabbath day. This is never an accident or coincidence in Jesus' ministry. It is a move deliberately designed to provoke a crisis, to force his adversaries to confront the real purpose of the Sabbath versus what the religious authorities had made of it.

Its real purpose? Rest. And rest equals not extra sleep and leisure, but above all peace with God, reconciliation, healing of the most important kind. Our afflictions, our sicknesses and infirmities, do not exist for the sole purpose of being taken away. They are not there in order for us to bide our time until they're gone (or we're gone). They sanctify. And the pain they introduce into our lives is the catalyst for growth that only God can bring about and only suffering can occasion.

It is also the only path we know to the glory yet to be revealed.

CHAPTER NINE
Upon a Watchtower I Stand: Fidelity in Waiting

Upon a watchtower I stand, O Lord, continually by day, and at my post I am stationed whole nights.

—ISAIAH 21:8

od can take away any problem he wishes, or hasten the end of any unpleasantness, which might leave us imagining a whole ungainly mess of wasted time in God's providence. Why not spare someone the time and trouble of being debilitated, down with illness, missing opportunities, and so forth? Haven't we all wondered this in the thick of a dark time? Haven't we all thought, *Lord, I've learned my lesson. Can't we move on now?*

Such a line of thinking betrays our focus, or rather our lack of focus on what is important. We look to many things, set our heart on many things, as the answers to present suffering or sorrow. As far as short-term solutions go, we seldom go wrong. My fever needs to return to normal body temperature; my anxiety needs to be pacified; my melancholy needs to be lifted by real joy. The fact that many people go wrong in seeking short-lived solutions to immediate problems is perhaps more a sign of desperation than vice or evil intent. We just want the problem gone.

But prolonged suffering seems only to absorb time and energy that could be more gainfully employed in some other direction. Again, we are back at the problem of focus. We look to productivity, getting things done with something to show for it, as a sign that all is well with us and the world. But that is a very shallow read on the rightness of reality. There is a type of blindness evidenced here, as Hubert van Zeller suggests, that is entirely manmade, a result of a distorted perspective, "a blindness brought about by staring at material objects seen out of focus."[1] When we look at the wrong things with defective lenses, or even the right things with warped vision, we see something that isn't there, but think it is. And how easily we set our hopes on the figment before us if it happens to correspond to our immediate need for relief.

As we endure day and night like the watchman in Isaiah, waiting for some sign of *something*, we need to know what to watch for. A sentinel knows the signs of enemy encroachment; a stargazer connects the dots in the night sky. A Christian,

1   Van Zeller, *Approach to Calvary*, 12.

commanded by the Lord to be vigilant at all times, should have facility in reading the signs of divine activity, especially when the time is prolonged and monotonous.

If Jesus is the Alpha and Omega, the beginning and the end, then everything in between must also be his. This is the truth enunciated by St. Paul, that for him "to live is Christ" (Phil 1:21). Thus our prayerful quest into life's "in between," the seeming wasteland of time and energy and accomplishment, must lead us back to Jesus. And really, before going on, we should stop and ask ourselves if we are on the same page as St. Paul. Is Christ our life? If he's not entirely our life, what fills the blank after "to live is…"? How we answer that global question also decides how we will answer our other major questions about love, suffering, meaning—all of the big questions in life.

If we begin with the principle that life in Christ is everything, then what befalls us in this world begins to appear as it truly is: various means for deeper and deeper union with God in Christ, means for fruit-bearing in him, means for growing in likeness to him. Our problem is that we do not see as God sees, and never will. We formulate a host of needs, preferences, and hopes that may or may not correspond to what God wills for us. Hence the perennial need for detachment. Hence the even more urgent need to trust. We cannot regularly hold out our wishes to be contradicted unless we trust the wisdom of the one who tells us no.

Jesus often speaks in his kingdom parables about small things becoming great over time. Seeds are sown, time passes, and they grow, if properly cared for. Then comes the harvest. A tree grows large enough to accommodate "the birds of the air" (see Lk 13:19). Things come to maturity in their own time, as Ecclesiastes says, "He has made everything beautiful in its time" (Eccl 3:11). It is fairly easy to apply this to the Church, since the Church is the kingdom of God on earth. Preaching repentance and forgiveness "to all nations, beginning from Jerusalem" is how Jesus maps out the apostles' missionary itinerary (see Lk 24:47).

But to make it personal is a more complicated business. God also has a plan for all of the small things in our lives— both the ones that try us and the ones that console us, the good and the bad. Not all things are equally important, but all have a place. Nothing is overlooked by God. Not a sparrow falls without his permission. Every hair and every grain of sand is numbered and accounted for (see Mt 10:29–30; Sir 1:2–10). *How* everything contributes to God's plan and to our sanctification is seldom clear to us, but it is certain that everything does.

Our hope is tested precisely in those areas where we cannot see, where we cannot have and hold what we want. We do not and cannot see the finished product, the fruit ripe for harvest, and we are instead made to wait. Perhaps a voice inside each of us says, *I can't just scatter the seed and wait.*

I can't just expect a tiny seed to become a tree. Inside each of us is a fallen person who isn't sure that the invisible God can be trusted. We fear surrendering into the hands of another whom we cannot see. We want to be trusting children of God, but when unexpected or sad events come about in our lives, or when nothing happens at all, being a child might not be our first response. But only those who have planted and waited can say, along with St. Paul, that "hope does not disappoint" (Rom 5:5). That is not a casual, easy comment. It comes from the mouth of those who faithfully went the distance with their Lord.

Called to Wait

Waiting is a kind of darkness. From a certain point of view, it is also a vocation. Religious who profess the vows of poverty, chastity, and obedience implicitly vow to wait. Natural human fulfillment typically involves marriage, self-determination, and private property sufficient for comfort and ease. Religious certainly have love, freedom, and a sufficiency for decent survival, but the immediate (and legitimate) gratification afforded by having one's own spouse, property, and so forth, sits permanently on hold while God makes himself the surety of our happiness. This side of heaven, our happiness is always incomplete, always has a longing about it, exacerbated (by design not defect) by the lack of the very things we've renounced for the sake of the kingdom.

Hubert van Zeller depicts a certain individual longing for the consummation of death learning the connection between darkness, delay, and vocation. Of all places, he learns it in the best: the fourteenth station of the Way of the Cross. He writes:

> A certain soul, in whom the longing for death was strong, but in whose desire were mingled motives of escape, was given interiorly to understand, while making the Stations of the Cross, that the fourteenth station represented his particular vocation: hidden with Christ in the tomb, and waiting. "I can bear the darkness," he said to our Lord, "but I cannot bear indefinitely waiting." "Then you cannot bear the darkness," came the answer, "because your waiting is your darkness."[2]

Starting Small

A very small seed that becomes a sheltering tree; a flat brown field slowly grows into golden wheat: shelter, safety, nourishment. God's kingdom is like that. In God's kingdom, little things go a long way. Do we want big solutions to our big problems? How about a small solution that grows over time and heals us in the process? How about slow growth over a long period of time, and the growth comes from something very small? And we don't understand how it happens. Or we

2   Hubert van Zeller, *The Inner Search* (New York: Sheed and Ward, 1957), 191–192.

don't see it happening. Doesn't that go against our preferences? Wouldn't we rather see immediate results?

Between the planting and the mature fruit, or the harvest, we have to wait. We have to do certain things over and over again—as the man who "should sleep and rise night and day" (Mk 4:26–29). Many are too impulsive to wait. They want to get things moving, to have what they want right away. That's our culture in a nutshell. The Lord most of the time says, *No, this slower way of painstaking cultivation and growth is better.*

In the last chapter, we spent a considerable amount of time with a blind man whose faith had grown in darkness for years. At this point, we can consider darkness and healing from another vantage point, from a pair of healings in the Gospel of Mark (Mk 7:31–37; 8:22–26). Again, a time lapse precedes the problem that needs remedy, but what happens upon healing underscores the issue at hand: all time is Christ's. The period we occupy in history must be looked at not in terms of realizing our ambitions and dreams before someone calls time-out, but in terms of walking at God's pace and following his lead.

When Jesus heals a a person who is deaf and mute and then a blind man in Mark's Gospel, he finds these men who are significantly closed off from the world around them. Dependent on others for guidance and information, the men cannot enjoy some of the most basic experiences that make life enjoyable: seeing, hearing, and speaking. Their lives seem to be more about what they *cannot* do than what they *can* do. And what is more, certain formative sense experiences for them will remain irretrievable—depending upon whether their disability appeared at birth or later. Their healing, in any event, is not retroactive. The past does not come back and they don't get back what they've missed.

With their healing, everything suddenly changes. Sunlight floods in, ears are immediately full of the sounds of voices, of birdsong, of children playing and crying. And the first thing either seen or heard is the face and voice of Jesus. And Jesus is smiling. And so are they—feeling like they've been born again. Whether they had the faculties of sight and hearing and then lost them is, again, not known and (now we can say) not even very important. Because we can be sure that having them restored by Christ was reward enough—not simply having them restored by some stroke of fortune, but by the hand of Christ. "Hand" meaning that the healing comes from Christ's will, his heart, his love. His touch in the midst of our pain makes up for every loss. The sacrifice of many years of frustrated communication, of having to be cared for by others, of feeling their way around, was all worth it for these men.

They do not get back the years of experiences they might have had, but instead receive a grace the magnitude of which outshines any loss they may have heretofore lamented. This might be a difficult truth to assimilate, that knowing

Christ makes up for everything—every loss, every pain, every suffering—without necessarily taking any of it away. Already we can hear St. Paul counting off the things he once considered gain but now considers less than nothing, compared to knowing the Lord:

> Indeed I count everything as loss because of the surpassing worth of knowing Christ Jesus my Lord. For his sake I have suffered the loss of all things, and count them as refuse, in order that I may gain Christ. (Phil 3:8)

Finding the Treasure

People who have experienced the presence of Christ in their lives in a transformative way are eager not only to count as "loss" their former goods, but are quite prepared to throw their excess cargo overboard. And they're in a hurry to do it! Zacchaeus makes generous overcompensation for his dishonesty, fishermen apostles abandon their nets, tax collectors leave behind lucrative jobs, disciples near and far say goodbye to family and friends—this is only the beginning of what saints will continue to do up to the present day for the sake of the surpassing worth of knowing Christ Jesus, their Lord. Jesus has this effect on people who are open to him. And he more than supplies for what we've let go, lost, or missed out on. After a while, it all seems like adding zeroes compared to the treasure they've discovered.

When Jesus compares his kingdom to a single rare pearl worth the cost of all we own, he is making the same point in parable form (see Mt 13:45–46). All that we lose, give up, or sell is found again in a better way in the one thing that is everything. The things we let go of do not come back, but are superseded by an even greater good—no longer a variety of personal belongings, but one thing only, the one thing necessary (see Lk 10:42).

Applying this truth to our own lives may be a painful but necessary means to our own inner healing. Of course, if we have not yet entered into a deep relationship with the Lord, all of this may have a simplistic or unrealistic ring to it. But think about the grief behind our regrets. What does it all point to? Regrettable relationships with parents, rejection by peers, a "defect" of body that made us less popular at school, sickness that prevented us from a golden opportunity, a friendship we could never pursue, medications we must take, feeling like we've been "typecast" in life, and so on. We've barely scratched the surface of human woes, and frankly have stayed mainly on the surface. Deeper wounds require special handling, and yet this does not change the point at hand: Every loss finds its balm in Christ.

And this is because all of our losses and regrets and sorrows point to the same thing: we all want to be loved, accepted, and valued for who we are. Anything that makes us feel rejected or undervalued leaves us feeling incomplete. We need to meet and be loved by One who reveals our true value in terms we never would have thought possible: the broken body and outpoured blood of Christ. We need to enter a relationship with one who can cleanse our guilt, set us free, and give our life new meaning and direction. People can get locked into ways of thinking and acting that issue from their woundedness and lead nowhere good. Life becomes all about waiting for the solution to come along or despairing of anything that can make things right. Resentment is ever loitering in the background.

The thought that our lives can actually not only take an entirely different direction, but even assume a fuller meaning is simply not entertained, and yet knowing the Lord makes both happen. We take along with us everything that we are, defects and all, and the Lord sets us on a different trajectory altogether. Outwardly, life might not change much, but the inner renewal will make our old world seem like a place newly created for living, living a new life in a new way.

All suffering is worthwhile that leads to Christ. Whether he heals the body or not is very secondary to the life-changing encounter with him. Jesus is more concerned that we have our sins forgiven than that we run around freely; he is more solicitous for a saved world, a world of redeemed and reconciled people, than for a race of healthy, flawless superheroes. In the end, his will is that both body and soul be joined together in perfection, but we may only find it in looking forward to the blessed hope of the resurrection at the end of time.

For the present, it is important to reflect on the unfulfilled, the waiting, the disappointments, the apparent pointlessness of not getting what we have legitimately sought in life. I think everyone over a certain age generates two categories of things: those that they would like to have restored and, on the other hand, those that they would like to have taken away.

What would we hope to have restored? If we could ask God for such a thing, what would it be? Time, youth, innocence, another chance to do or say something that we got wrong the first time around? Second chances, missed opportunities, squandered resources, broken relationships—if we could only get those back; if they could only be restored.

People also have things they want to have taken away: regrets, guilt, ailments of the body, ailments of the mind, difficult relationships. We carry these things day in and day out, and we believe we would be happier and relieved if they were gone. It is easy to say that God has a purpose for everything in our lives, that nothing is unforeseen by him, even the things we regret; it is both easy and true to say it. But when we don't see that purpose, when we're tempted to curse the darkness, and when giving up seems the best option, then what do we have to say about God's purposes?

God pushes some people to the point of crisis: Job, Abraham, Jonah, and Simon Peter come to mind. They were on the point of going crazy from a feeling of abandonment, feeling like they were on a wild goose chase. They became angry, panicky, and fearful—God allowed them to go through all of that, and they weren't always equal to the challenge. They suffered unsuccessfully at times. They complained. But to us they are holy Job, Abraham our Father in Faith, Jonah the Prophet, St. Peter.

The failures of the holy ones to endure their trials seamlessly contains important information about God and about the true character of human holiness. We learn that we don't need to bring back the past, to have another shot at that missed opportunity—nor do we need to have all of our burdens taken away. We need to find God in our mistakes, brokenness, failure, immaturity, impatience, and so on, because that is where God meets his friends.

The one who stands day and night on the watchtower waits mostly in silence and inactivity; at least, his outward stance would suggest that. But his eyes are open; he is on the alert. He sounds the alarm if trouble approaches or opens the gates to an ally. What an image of the faithful soul. "The whole life of a good Christian is a holy desire," says St. Augustine. He later continues, "Let us stretch ourselves unto [the Lord], that when He shall come, He may fill us."[3] St. Augustine further

3   Augustine of Hippo, *Homily 4 on the First Epistle of John*, in *Nicene and Post-Nicene Fathers: First Series*, Vol. 7, trans. H. Browne, ed. Philip Schaff (Buffalo, NY: Christian Literature Publishing Co., 1888), no. 6. Edited for New Advent website by Kevin Knight: https://www.newadvent.org/fathers/170204.htm.

says that this desire is the "duty" of those who cannot yet see, cannot yet apprehend, what they long for. Thus, "God, by deferring our hope, stretches our desire; by the desiring, stretches the mind; by stretching, makes it more capacious."[4]

Christian life equals holy desire. And desire means wanting something badly—either something we don't have or something we only have a part of and want all of it. Those who stand sentry duty, waiting for Christ, cannot afford to be ruminating on past losses, distracting themselves from hoping in the Lord. Their job is to kindle a fire. Then when their Savior comes he will find his servants not poking dead ashes, but fostering flames that reach to heaven.

4   Augustine of Hippo, *Homily 4 on the First Epistle of John*, no. 6.

CHAPTER TEN
Songs in the Night

Where is God my Maker, who gives songs in the night?

—JOB 35:10

t. Cyprian of Carthage (ca. 210-258) paid striking tribute to some of his fellow Christians detained in prison, awaiting their martyrdom. Their holding cells, he claimed, constituted a "darkness brighter than the sun itself, more resplendent than this light of the world."[1] The bright darkness comes from the fact that God is filling them with his presence, just as he fills any temple dedicated to his glory. The prisoners are those temples, especially sanctified (as St. Cyprian continues) by their praise of God.

The image of the incarcerated singing in their chains brings to mind St. Paul and St. Silas locked up in the "inner prison" with their feet in stocks, singing praise to God at

---

1 Cyprian of Carthage, Ep. 6, 1–2: CSEL 3, 480–482,in *Liturgy of the Hours*, vol. 3, 1686.

midnight: "But about midnight Paul and Silas were praying and singing hymns to God, and the prisoners were listening to them" (Acts 16:25). The setting is incongruous with sung prayer—with praise especially. Urgent but silent prayer in detention, no one would question. But to get so vocal that others can hear, in circumstances so gloomy and desperate, suggests a power at work that transcends even the most hostile environments. And that power is the Holy Spirit, the first mover of all prayer, the initiator of praise, the author of confidence in God.

Praise of God in our darkness, even with death in sight, is a sure sign that the Holy Spirit has found warm reception in our souls. Although we might still feel cold and abandoned, the Spirit insists that we are children who compel a hearing from on High. God is listening and *blessing* as we lift up our voices at times and places normally inhospitable to prayer.

What good is our prayer, our spiritual life, if it only functions when the atmosphere is ideal enough for it? If we can only find God in the midst of pews and candles, we will be forgetful of God in the majority of places we need to be on a daily basis. The Holy Spirit will need to get our attention by force, so to speak, if we are not otherwise listening vigilantly to his promptings. The Spirit of Truth whom the world cannot receive, but who nevertheless nimbly wends through the ways of the world, speaks, sighs, and sings in the soul of the vigilant Christian.

Songs, even in the night, are no strange thing for him. If David said, "At midnight I rise to praise thee" (Ps 119:62), and "I think of thee upon my bed, and meditate on thee in the watches of the night" (Ps 63:6), then surely the same Spirit who inspired his words listens when we take them on our lips, day or night.

Doubtless, the same psalms that exhort us to praise God in the heights, in broad daylight, do not forbid praise in the depths and in the dark of night. Some spend a considerable amount of time in the lowlands of the spirit. But as we have said elsewhere in this book, the saints show us how powerfully God can reach us, even in the lowest, most hidden and wretched of places. And it goes both ways: the saints likewise reveal how near at hand the Lord is to those who call upon him, wherever they find themselves.

Fruit of the Spirit

The Savior is prophetically commissioned by God to "open the eyes that are blind, to bring out the prisoners from the dungeon, from the prison those who sit in darkness" (Is 42:7). And when he commands "Come forth," and "Appear," to "those who are in darkness," the prisoners do indeed come forth (Is 49:9). Jesus can infiltrate our lockdown and make light shine there, even making us feel perfectly free in confinement. This is a gift of his Spirit and not merely the reward of self-discipline.

The fruit of the Spirit listed by St. Paul ("love, joy, peace, patience, kindness, goodness, faithfulness, gentleness, self-control" [Gal 5:22–23]) become especially operative for saintly Christians when, humanly speaking, no good reason exists for joy, peace, and all the rest. Such souls can sing at any time, in any circumstance, because the Holy Spirit has opened their eyes to see the goodness of God, a goodness that dazzles the thickest darkness, as angels flooded the midnight sky of Christmas with radiance and song.

If there is one disciple most fruitful and holy in every way, in whom the Holy Spirit has free reign, full range of voice, and is limitless and expansive like the wind, it is the Holy Mother of God.

She, the Mother of the Light of the World, is one who like dawn heralds the daylight, who proclaims the fidelity of God when all promises seem forgotten and the future appears lost. It has always been very natural for the Church's liturgy to apply the words of the Song of Solomon to Our Lady, reckoning her a light in her own right: "Who is this that looks forth like the dawn, fair as the moon, bright as the sun, terrible as an army with banners?" (Song 6:10). Solomon wonders at such beauty, so awe-inspiring that it freezes him in his tracks and makes him gape with amazement. The Blessed Virgin Mary is this beauty: the refulgence of Christ, a mirror in which his light is permanently captured and brandished to the glory of God's grace.

All that we've said thus far in this chapter about light defying its surroundings, shining "out of context," finds its human embodiment in the Mother of God. And it is to her that we turn in concluding these reflections, especially as she is showcased in the liturgy of Advent. Advent, coinciding with the darkest time of year seasonally, is really her season, the season of the Mother whose time is at hand. And it bears all of the themes we have tried to develop in these pages. No matter how dark, cold, wet, or frozen the days, the Church annually insists that we contemplate the lightsome figure of the Blessed Virgin as she listens, responds, and journeys in anticipation of Christ's entry into the world. Every year, she is like springtime breaking in through the gray days of December.

The Advent liturgy never lets us forget Our Lady's presence and prominence, perhaps especially in the Liturgy of the Hours. Each of the daily antiphons for the minor hours of midmorning, midday, and midafternoon announce her as the Mother of the Messiah, record the archangel Gabriel's message to her, and show her pondering that message of divine motherhood within a virginal life. The liturgy ensures that, even for the space of a few hours, we forget her not.

The Eucharistic liturgy begins to follow her movements in earnest in the latter part of the season, with readings recounting the Annunciation, Visitation, and other events in which she is influential, if not actually present. And what does the Blessed Virgin Mary have to tell us? What is her message to those not only in a dark season, but in life's dark depths? She listens.

> My beloved speaks and says to me: "Arise, my love, my fair one, and come away; for lo, the winter is past, the rain is over and gone. The flowers appear on the earth, the time of singing has come." (Song 2:10–12)

Once again, the Church puts these words on the lips of Our Lady.[2] And she begins by telling us what she has heard. Is this not important to note? Listening precedes acting, loving, praying—doing anything worthwhile in the service of God. Are we prepared to listen like Our Lady? To take in what we cannot yet comprehend, and to trust that what is said to us comes from the Beloved? Listening in winter indoors, as it were, to a voice outside assuring us that the snow has melted, the rain had done its work, and the earth is coming alive beneath our feet—this is to hear the voice of the Beloved urging us to live, to love, to rejoice, and to praise.

It is the Messiah telling us to come forth, appear, and stand in the sunlight. We are being put on notice that "the time of singing has come." Did we know that? Isn't that good news? Isn't that gospel to our ears?

The mystery of the Visitation forms the setting par excellence for a sort of New Testament "Song of Solomon"

---

2 See the liturgy for December 21, which features as first reading the Song of Songs 2:8-14, whose sentiments are applied to Mary in tandem with the Gospel of the Visitation.

(see Lk 1:39–56). It is sung by one who has the right to sing it, since Our Lady proclaims in the Magnificat that the battle is already won. Spring has come and will never again lapse into winter.

Owing to her Immaculate Conception, she began even her prenatal existence as one in whom Christ had already conquered sin, original and actual. And this means that both her character and personality were distinguished by unfailing humility and gratitude. She is completely God's masterwork, and knows it. In a related context, Our Lady is known affectionately in Santa Fe, New Mexico, as *La Conquistadora*, a militant-sounding title that yet bespeaks a prior conquest of the soul: she who has already been conquered by God, conquers souls in turn for him. This is the pattern of discipleship and apostolate for every Christian: "In all these things we are more than conquerors through him who loved us" (Rom 8:37).

Our Lady celebrates a spiritual triumph that, let us not forget, was as incongruous as St. Paul and St. Silas' midnight worship. Think of the historical setting of the Magnificat: the very earth upon which the Blessed Virgin Mary stands and sings is spoken for, occupied by Roman forces. Yet with her feet firmly planted on Judean soil, she lets loose her canticle of praise. Doesn't she know that her people are more or less renting their own homeland from pagans? What right has she to praise the Lord? If the psalmist plaintively asks, "How shall we sing the Lord's song in a foreign land?" (Ps 137:4), could not Our Lady just as easily say, "How shall I sing of the Lord as a foreigner in my own land?"

But there is a presence inside of the Blessed Virgin Mary teaching her how to sing, how to rejoice. And he inspires her to tell us and all generations what the mystery of the Incarnation means: God in Christ reclaims the world by redeeming it. The firstborn of all creation is not only the One *through whom* all things were made but *for whom* they all exist. Both Our Lady and St. Elizabeth freely testify to this with praise and thanksgiving, as though victory has just been claimed and will never again be reversed. They embody what we hear from Isaiah at Christmas:

> Thou hast multiplied the nation, thou hast increased its joy; they rejoice before thee as with joy at the harvest, as men rejoice when they divide the spoil. For the yoke of his burden, and the staff for his shoulder, the rod of his oppressor, thou hast broken. (Is 9:3–4)

Although Roman procurators, centurions, and legions administer their homeland as just another province of the Roman empire, notice that the holy Virgin and her holy cousin rejoice in the Lord, unburdened by the occupation of their land. The truly important things happen within them and cannot be diminished by the unideal setting. It is the reality during which God takes flesh and visits his people. It is a darkness or twilight about to be invaded by the Light of the World. One from heaven has come to cast fire on the earth, even the earth on which they stand. Once again, the Holy Spirit stirs to kindle joy and praise.

When St. Elizabeth praises her, the Blessed Virgin Mary tells her cousin what is happening on the inside: she is magnifying, praising, glorifying the Lord. She is free to do this, uncompromised by fears, resentments or curiosity about her future. Can we say the same for ourselves? What are our souls doing right now? Are they sorrowful, fearful, apprehensive? Is something holding back our praise? If we want to share in their hymn of victory and praise, if we want to sing with the Mother of God, must we, too, be unburdened?

The Lord Takes Us as We Are

I think of how I, as a priest and religious, daily take the Magnificat on my lips at Vespers, sometimes still weighed down by the day's events. I start to rejoice, but then recall something I said earlier that I shouldn't have said; I remember something I did many years ago that I would like to take back or redo, but can't; and so my rejoicing stops before it can even start. Then I think of future problems—tomorrow's or next year's—which again blocks my joy. The enemy is ever lurking, insinuating, *What right do you have to rejoice?*

St. Teresa of Avila says that in our lives,

we are occupied in our pastimes, business affairs, pleasures, and worldly buying and selling, and still falling into sin and rising again. [...] Yet [our] Lord desires intensely that we love Him and seek His company, so much so that from time to time He calls us to draw near [to] Him.[3]

The whole variety of daily human experience is accounted for here. But note how quickly she assures us that the Lord still calls us to intimacy. It is a liberating truth that the Lord will take us as we are, with whatever goodwill we have, and welcome us to his side, even if our mind and affections are still working to disengage from worldly cares. Jesus' mission did not include the removal of all foreign troops from Palestine, nor was the establishment of a just society a precondition of his ministry. Nor was any other ideal set of circumstances prerequisite for his preaching the gospel. Doesn't this tell us how willing he is to work with the best and the worst we have to offer him?

That is perhaps a long way of illustrating a simple spiritual point. If when we come to prayer the body feels tired, the mind struggles to focus, and if we are responsible for many and weighty things and are therefore generally exhausted and distracted, isn't it for such people that Jesus was born? Didn't he come for exhausted and distracted people like ourselves? "The Lord God has given me the tongue of those who are

---

3   Teresa of Avila, *Interior Castle*, in *The Collected Works of St. Teresa of Avila*, vol. 2, trans. Kieran Kavanaugh, OCD, and Otilio Rodriguez, OCD (Washington, DC: ICS, 1987), 2.1.2, 298.

taught," the Messiah says, "that I may know how to sustain with a word him that is weary" (Is 50:4). The one who speaks to our weariness is the Lord. He recognizes it for what it is; he does not pretend it isn't there. He ever invites the weary and burdened to himself.

Nor is he unaware of how trapped we can feel indoors while inclement winter threatens at the shutters. But trapped is not how the Blessed Virgin feels or acts. From one point of view, everyone in Judea, Galilee, and the surrounding regions labors under oppression. However good and orderly an occupying force may be, it is still an intrusive, unwelcome presence. Walking in holy Mary's footsteps, we might find ourselves resenting the politics of the day, fearing the violence of the periodic uprisings and their brutal suppression, becoming bitter over the disloyalty of so many fellow countrymen collaborating with the Romans and Herodians.

Does the Blessed Virgin Mary's demeanor reflect any of this? Does her song have anything other than a tone of triumph? She is singing in the night, pitch perfect. She is nowhere close to ignorant about conditions in her homeland. But someone greater than it all justifies a song of praise—yes, greater than Solomon, greater than the temple, greater than anyone or anything that had come before or could come after. When someone possesses God so securely, when someone's roots are inextricably fixed in him, one doesn't need to wait around for better times before saying, "My spirit rejoices in

God my Savior!" The body might ache, the mind be troubled, but in the depths of the soul, one can yet rise to praise the goodness of God.

> Yea, thou dost light my lamp; the Lord my God lightens my darkness.
>
> Yea, by thee I can crush a troop; and by my God I can leap over a wall.
>
> This God—his way is perfect; the promise of the Lord proves true;
>
> he is a shield for all those who take refuge in him.
>
> For who is God, but the Lord? And who is a rock, except our God?—the God who girded me with strength, and made my way safe. (Ps 18:28–32)

In certain seasons of life, the thought might occur to us: *In another lifetime, I could have done this or that; in another lifetime, I could have pursued that career, that relationship; in another lifetime, I could have taken an entirely different path. And where would I be right now had I done that?* Our Lady is here to tell us that, however young or old we are, we only get one life. And it is good, wherever it is lived, if lived with and for the Lord.

The fantasy of another life running parallel to this one, a more ideal or perfect life, needs to be firmly rejected by those who believe in the Incarnation of the Son of God. Just as the Lord Jesus became man at the end of a very long road through human and salvation history, yet it was one road. And his life on earth was one life. And looking at it from the outside, it was mostly a boring life. But from the inside, it was an entirely different story. Monotonous and boring perhaps to dull eyes, but at a deeper level, rich, fruitful, and full of love and joy because it was full of divine life.

When we become adults, we have to face the challenges and heartbreaks of adult life; we can't return to the sandbox and pretend. We can't make-believe that things are not as they are. We see evil, experience evil, and commit sin, and we must be constantly seeking mercy and healing. Thoughts of escape, the tuning out of reality at least, in fantasy, can rush upon us when life seems fruitless and wearisome.

What maestro could possibly get us to raise our voices from the rut of routine? It always amazes me how monastic life does all of this on purpose—the sameness of the regular life intertwined with the hours of the Divine Office. That's right: boring on purpose. And just as right and deliberate: praise of God at ironclad intervals. Seven times a day, monastery churches fill with monks, nuns, or canons—having come from their manual work, their silence, their daily duties which seldom vary. Why does this life exist in the Church? A life that seems to embody the very frustrations that make people want to run from their tedium? Does it proclaim a message to the rest of the faithful?

Yes. And it is a Marian message. We don't have to feel trapped. Once God has become deeply real to us, he sets us free to grow in those very circumstances that had made us feel trapped. You could say that religious in monasteries "trap" themselves on purpose to do what Moses told the Israelites to do: "Fear not, stand firm, and see the salvation of the Lord. [...] You have only to be still" (Ex 14:13–14). Once again, we are back in the prison cell, singing hymns with St. Paul, St. Silas, St. Gregory the Illuminator, St. Maximilian Kolbe, Ven. Francis-Xavier Nguyễn Văn Thuận, and so on. God can so burrow into the soul as to make even a cell a bountiful "place of springs" (Ps 84:6).

The frustrations and stress of life will likely still be there, but when our lives are totally in God's hands, we find strength to see our way through them, at least to accept the things we cannot change and grow from them.

Many do not see turning to God as increasing their freedom. Following, surrender, obedience: these all sound terribly restricting. And in some respects, this is true. But it is unrealistic to claim we serve no one, are obedient to no one, in not serving and obeying God. We are always following some principle, striving for some goal or ideal, whether we identify it as such or not. Humans have no other choice but to act in this way. We are hardwired to act for an end, to adhere to principles or ideals. And in these ways, we willingly limit ourselves, without faulting ourselves for excluding other possibilities.

As a wise old pastor once told me about balancing the demands of priestly ministry: "Father, when you say yes to one thing, you always have to say no to something else." In a nutshell, that is the rule of human choice: in admitting one thing we inevitably exclude another. It comes down to saying yes to the right things. And what is ultimately right for us is to choose for the sake of our ultimate goal, our final end. And this we call God.

The mystery of the Annunciation, perhaps the quintessential Advent mystery, makes us ask: *When God comes into my life, what happens to my freedom? Do I become less human in submitting to a will other than my own?* Well, what happened to Our Lady's freedom when the angel came to her? If it were possible, it expanded even beyond the already perfect freedom of one devoid of original or actual sin. That is, her willingness to say a wholehearted yes to God enabled her to enjoy both virginal integrity and the additional fulfillment of motherhood. Only God can so enlarge human freedom as to embrace such contraries as virginity and motherhood.

This privilege is obviously unique to the Blessed Virgin Mary, but the principle behind it is not. For all who surrender to the Lord, there exists a power uniting human limitations with an unimaginable divine plan. It is St. Paul's struggle and epiphany all over again: "I besought the Lord about this, [...] but he said to me, 'My grace is sufficient for you, for my power is made perfect in weakness.' I will all the more gladly boast of my weaknesses, that the power of

Christ may rest upon me" (2 Cor 12:8–9). God's plan for each of us requires humble submission to a light that only faith can follow. And it is in that submission that we find the real richness of life lived in God. All of the short-term projects and choices that—we imagine—are so expressive of our individuality and personal liberty, all of the sad limitations that glare at us like wardens: all lose their power to trap us once we have given our heart to God. Then real living and true freedom begin.

Fr. Bede Jarrett, OP, describes the consequences of the eye-opening caused by our submission to God and especially to the Holy Spirit. More than a change in outlook, life itself is transformed in our concrete choices and actions.

> The Vision has come; it cannot simply open my eyes to new things in life without thereby altering that very life itself. Not only shall I find that what seemed to me before to be evil now appears to me to be a blessing; but on that very account what before I tried to avoid, or, having got, tried to be rid of, I shall now accept, perhaps even seek. Similarly, whereas then I was weak, now I am strong; and increase of strength means new activities, new energy put into the old work and finding its way out into works altogether new. My emotions, finally, which [imperiled] and dominated my life, slip now into a subordinate position, and while thereby as actively employed as before, are held under discipline. It is clear, therefore, that the gifts will not leave me

where I was before, but will influence my actions as well as alter my vision.[4]

In the most practical and helpful fashion, Fr. Jarrett summarizes the daily difference that God's active presence in our lives makes: when we are intentional in our surrender to God, all of the things that formerly held us back and made life tough going, not to mention miserable, are reversed into minor conquests. Growth springs up when we see life, not as negotiating a total wasteland, but as managing the mixed field that Christ says it is (see Mt 13: 24–30). With the weeds and wheat trying each other, a more robust harvest is finally produced not in spite of the jumble but because it is not removed.

If we have taken some wrong turns in coping with life's difficulties, trying to get out from under our burdens or to slough them off entirely and escape, Our Lady lays the simple truth before us, preaching without *preaching*: surrendering to God is the only way to be made free and whole. Committed entirely to God, she is not trapped, but comfortably at home.

Allow the sound of the Blessed Virgin Mary's greeting to enter your ears, as St. Elizabeth did. Allow her greeting to inspire the same joy and praise. Don't resist it. *Peace*, Our Lady says. *Peace, my sister. Peace, my cousin. For I bring you glad*

4   Bede Jarrett, OP, *The Abiding Presence of the Holy Ghost in the Soul* (Westminster, MD: The Newman Bookshop, 1918). Project Gutenberg website: : https:// www.gutenberg.org/files/34855/34855-h/34855-h.htm

tidings of great joy: "The winter is past, the rain is over and gone. The flowers appear on the earth, the time of singing has come" (Song 2:11–12).

Therefore, sing to the Lord this new song. The old song belongs to the faded winter. The new song is the canticle of those always being born. Only the living can sing. Only those in love, says St. Augustine, have something to sing about.[5] Even as we feel the weakness of our flesh and perhaps strain in the mind, let us sing from a deeper place within—from that place where God dwells, living and reigning, conquering and teaching us how to conquer.

The Light shines in the darkness, our darkness, the world's darkness, and the darkness cannot overcome it.

---

5 Augustine of Hippo, Sermon 336, 1–PL 38, 1472.